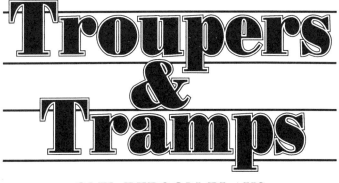

Troupers & Tramps

ONE-PERSON PLAYS

Rachael C. Burchard

Music by Dana Libonati

Meriwether Publishing Ltd.
Colorado Springs, Colorado

Meriwether Publishing Ltd., Publisher
P.O. Box 7710
Colorado Springs, CO 80933

Editor: Arthur L. Zapel
Typesetting: Susan Trinko
Cover design: Tom Myers
Cover photo: Sarah Foltz

NOTICE FOR PROFESSIONAL PRODUCTION
For any form of non-amateur presentation (professional stage, radio or
television), permission must be obtained in writing from the publisher,
Meriwether Publishing Ltd. (address above).

Library of Congress Cataloging-in-Publication Data

Burchard, Rachael C.
     Troupers and tramps : one person plays / by Rachael C. Burchard. --
  1st ed.
       p.   cm.
     ISBN 1-56608-001-0
     1. Monologues.   [1. Monologues.]   I. Title
  PS3552.U64T76   1993
  812'.54--dc20   93-38914
                                                    CIP
                                                     AC

For
Ethel Sargent Warberg Chandler

ACKNOWLEDGMENTS

The author gratefully acknowledges the assistance and cooperation of Shirley Adams, Judy Ashley, Cecily Ballenger, Tricia Ballenger, Gina Burchard, Margot Burchard, Petrea Burchard, Stuart Burchard, Jerald Fairbanks, JoAnne Fox, Joecille Fulham, Norman Goss, Virginia Jordan, Marilynn Karbonski, Donna Millar, LaVonne Mueller, Olga Petrovich, Jessie Snook, the Wordwrights and MacWriters.

A premier performance of nine of the plays from *Troupers and Tramps* and three from *We the Real People I* and *II* under title, *Saints and Clowns*, was performed by Gallery Players of Oregon on October 1, 2, 3, 8, 9, 1993, at McMinnville, Oregon, under the direction of Joanne Walker. The actors were Meredith Michaud, Melissa Plumeau, Jackie Groth, Jane Maddox, Diana Lee, Liz Crouch, Jane Nielsen, Win Dolan, Jonny Hofmann, Ken Moore, and Myron LeRoy.

The people depicted in these plays are strictly imaginary and not based on real persons, living or dead.

PREFACE

The one-person plays in *Troupers and Tramps* are designed for flexibility of performance and variety in acting experience. They can be used one at a time for dinner theatre, contest, or audition or, in a selected grouping, for a full-length performance. An all-woman show can be arranged easily from the thirteen selections for women. Some numbers can be performed by physically handicapped actors. Themes may be carried out through selection of pieces dealing with personal identity, teenage issues, or celebration of the human spirit.

The music composed by Dana Libonati for the collection provides an overture and between-act bridges, eliminating awkward interludes which are a hazard in the production with numerous short scenes.

The creative director will enjoy the chance to select the appropriate roles for a cast of varied talents from singing to gymnastics, and the actors will experience the challenge of creating a unique character without the competition or compromise sometimes required when other actors are involved. One-to-one schedules for actor and director can simplify rehearsals and save time.

The need for a new term to identify one-person plays like these prompts my suggestion of *apostroplay*. Neither monolog, monodrama nor soliloquy is quite accurate. Monolog suggests a speech by one person to listeners who do not respond, but it usually refers to an excerpt from a longer play or stand-up comedy. Monodrama, aside from sounding like a disease or at best a bad mood, is a drama to be acted by a single person, but the term does not suggest brevity or allow for comedy. In soliloquy the actor speaks directly to the audience to tell them what he or she is thinking, but does not usually speak to another character in the play, absent or present.

Apostrophe, aside from suggesting abbreviation, is "the addressing of a person usually not present or of a thing usually personified for rhetorical purposes." *(Webster's Third New International Dictionary)* Holman and Harmon, editors of the sixth edition of *A Handbook to Literature*, expand upon the definition: "A figure of speech in which someone (usually but not always absent), some abstract quality, or a nonexistent personage is directly addressed as though present."

But "apostrophe" is not adequate to designate the brief play complete with plot, conflict, resolution, and stage action — all for one actor.

The compound, "apostroplay," provides the needed term for the one-person play. It combines the concepts of brevity, speech by one person to someone not present, and the dramatic unit of a play.

Here then, are apostroplays for actors — sensitive people who have discovered that the best way to understand other people is to play their roles, speak their words, and hear what they have to say. Here are apostroplays for one person to perform.

TABLE OF CONTENTS

Women Characters

Meredith Michaud as "ANNIE ANON"

1. ANNIE ANON

PRODUCTION NOTES

SET: Empty stage representing a road-side park.

LIGHTS: Daylight. Noon.

SOUND: No sound effects are needed.

PROPS: A fairly good bicycle for a girl. It must have a basket mounted over front tire — preferably a shallow wire one so that audience can see into it. In the basket are a well-worn teddy bear and a paper lunch sack complete with half an egg salad sandwich, a cookie, and an apple.

COSTUME: Annie, a thirteen-year-old girl, is pregnant. She will need well-designed and anchored padding to suggest full-term pregnancy. She wears maternity shorts and a top that looks as little-girlish as possible, preferably one with yoke smocking. The color should be becoming to the actor. She carries a large scarf, not necessarily coordinated in color, and wears well-worn flat shoes other than contemporary "running shoes."

PLAYING TIME: Eight or nine minutes.

CAST: One character, thirteen-year-old Annie Anon, and one bit player, a well-worn teddy bear named Grandpa, make up the cast.

AT RISE: As lights come up quickly, Annie appears Upstage Left on her bicycle which she is half riding, half walking. She is talking to the teddy bear in her bike basket. She stops at more or less Downstage Center and, picking up the bear, dismounts slowly.

1   Let's stop for awhile, Grandpa. I'm pooped. Lard Hips
2   can't see us this far from Wayward House anyway. Get some
3   exercise, she says to all of us. Get your exercise, girls. At least
4   I got one of the good bikes today. Wouldn't it be neat to have
5   one like this for our very own? You and me could go on picnics
6   or down to McDonald's — if we ever had a dollar. *(She takes the*
7   *scarf and sack from the basket, heavily lets herself to the floor, sits,*
8   *little-girl fashion, and lays out the lunch on the scarf. She eats as she*
9   *speaks, imitating each character she quotes.)*
10   At least we are eating. I have to say that much for
11   Wayward. They understand about eating. Better than Benstraps'
12   or Olenfords'. Wasn't that weird? Skim milk and plain toast —
13   one slice — for breakfast, one slice of bologna and crackers for
14   lunch. And supper, beans: beans baked, beans boiled, beans
15   fried and refried. You'd think we were sent there instead of jail
16   or something the way Mom Benstrap talked. "Be glad there's
17   food on the table," she says. "Be glad the state cares enough
18   to give you beans and a bed." That was before she takes off
19   with Benny to McDonald's. I'm already in bed in the porch.
20   Well, usually. Little Benny knew how to get his mommy's
21   money's worth out of me. "Use my bed," he says. "Warmer than
22   one of the cots on the porch." I wonder which one of the girls
23   he's keeping warm now. All loving and gentle, like, calling them
24   little sister. "Give me a hug, little sister. I'll keep you warm."
25   The creep.
26   Here, want a bite? Egg salad sandwich, apple, cookie. Nice,
27   after bologna and crackers for a year. *(She slowly changes*
28   *positions, places the bear into sitting position facing her, "feeds" him,*
29   *snuggles him. She is a child handling a child's security toy one*
30   *moment, a troubled young woman the next. She folds the sack into the*
31   *shape of a chef's or a baker's hat and puts it on the bear.)*
32   You look neat in a hat. You be a baker, and we'll eat all
33   the time! Here, have a bite of cookie, Mister Baker. Someday
34   we'll have a cookie jar for you, Grandpa. And a warm bed we
35   don't have to share with Benny Rat Trap. Remember way back

1   to Crawfords? They was really different. I had a crib, sort of.
2   They called me Annie, remember? Mom Crawford said I
3   was really, like legally, Annie Anon. *(A-non´)* She said the state
4   give me that name, Annie Anon. But the Makesmiths said I had
5   to go by their name. Then I was Ann Makesmith. I like Annie
6   Anon better; it's me. *(During the following speeches, she gets up,*
7   *wanders about kicking imaginary rocks, plucking imaginary weeds,*
8   *playing hopscotch.)*
9   If you could talk, you would tell me. My real name. You
10 even remember my real mom, don't you? Mom Crawford used
11 to tell me stories. One of them was about us, I think. About this
12 bear and baby sleeping together in a boot box. Remember? A
13 new bear and a new baby. And somebody left the boot box on
14 the steps at the agency and snuck away. The bear couldn't tell
15 them nothing, and the baby tried, but they thought all she was
16 doing was crying. Yeah, I think Mom Crawford told that one
17 about us. You and me in a boot box when they found us. But
18 somebody had to put us there.
19   Ouch ... *(She holds her belly in pain.)* I wonder what she
20 was like. I wonder if she had her own bike. I wonder if she
21 knew her mom. She probably didn't really want to give us away,
22 you know. If she had me and give me a teddy bear, I mean. She
23 give me you, Grandpa, so that there was something from the
24 very beginning.
25   Was she thirteen, like me, or a real mom already? Older,
26 I mean. Maybe even had a house or apartment? Maybe more
27 kids? Do you suppose we have real brothers and sisters
28 somewhere? Nah. Course not. She wouldn't give away just one
29 of her kids. Musta been like me — got no choice.
30   Only Lard Hips says we do have a choice. She says that
31 to Carrie, anyway. Of course Carrie has a mom right now. Her
32 mom will help bring up her baby if that's what they decide to
33 do. But can you imagine Mom Benstrap bringing up mine? She
34 won't even let me come back. "Influence on Benny." You heard
35 her. I'm an influence on Benny. No way would she take in my

1   baby — her own grandchild. No way I'd let her. Bitch.

2   I guess I don't blame her. A baby is for a long time. A long,
3   long time. You're too old to ride a bike before the baby grows
4   up. And I guess real moms don't talk to teddy bears. Well, I
5   ain't gonna be a real mom, then, because I gotta talk to you. I
6   gotta talk to somebody who knows about everything.
7   Beginnings.

8   And you don't eat much. That's another thing. Babies gotta
9   eat. For years and years. How are you and me gonna feed a
10   baby? And where are we all gonna sleep? And a baby's gotta
11   have blankets and things. Grandpa, what are we going to do?

12   I could've had the abortion. But who was gonna pay? It
13   costs a lot to go to the clinic and all. Nobody to pay for it.
14   Besides, I'd feel funny about that. Startin' a real baby and all.
15   No, I didn't want to do that. Somebody good will have to adopt
16   her. Somebody will want her. Him. It could be a him except
17   that there was my mom and then me, and I bet it's gonna be a
18   girl. If it was a boy it wouldn't ever have a baby. I couldn't be
19   so lucky. It'll be a girl. That's OK, I guess. I like being a girl,
20   except for taking the rap all the time. If I have a girl I don't
21   want her to take the rap like me. Live with a jillion foster
22   parents. Never know.

23   Grandpa, I gotta keep her! I gotta keep her so she'll always
24   have a mom! Have the name I give her. Know where she come
25   from.

26   If somebody adopts her, she'll never know us. Course she
27   might have her own bike. Wow. Maybe even a room with one
28   of those canopy beds like in Sears. Pink! *(She visualizes it.)* **And**
29   maybe they would buy her new jeans and running shoes.
30   Wouldn't it be neat to have new Levis and new blue Nikes? And
31   a real mom with her hair all poufed? Maybe even a dad?

32   We could maybe get her a teddy bear.

33   But no boot box. Boot boxes are definitely out.

34   Did you get enough to eat? Good. Come on. We better get
35   back to Wayward. We got some thinkin' to do. *(She maneuvers*

the bike into position, steps over the bar, seats the bear in the basket,
rocking the bike back and forth as she thinks.)

But how can I buy her a bear? *(There is a long silence. She*
reveals that the thought has come to her to give away this bear.)

No, Grandpa. No, I won't do it. I don't appreciate your
suggestion. You are old, real crappy. They'd stash you first
thing. I meant new. A new bear. And I still need to talk to you.
I won't do it. Yes, I love her. It's my stomach she kicks. I don't
care if my real mom did give you to me so that there was
something — I won't give you away. We gotta think of
something else. We gotta do this better than my mom did. *(There*
is another long silence in which she rocks back and forth on the bike,
studying the bear intently. She is facing audience.)

I could give you a sort of bath, I guess. And find a piece
of ribbon for your neck or something. *(After another silence, she*
slowly unfolds the scarf and flattens it in the bike basket. She rocks
the bear lovingly, touching its face. She gives it a long, slow hug. She
is a young mother preparing to give up her baby. She then wraps the
bear in the scarf as if wrapping a package and resolutely places it in
the basket. She turns the bike away from audience and rides it off
Upstage as lights dim.)

2. ANGELA

PRODUCTION NOTES

SET: A teenager's bedroom. The set can be done in detail, but the only essentials are a large chair or wheelchair and a small table.

LIGHTS: Soft. Evening, interior. Soft spot may be used.

SOUND: No background sound is necessary.

PROPS: The actor needs a blanket or afghan, a pillow, a tape recorder with microphone, and a large stuffed toy such as a turtle, giraffe, or dinosaur.

COSTUME: Angela wears a nightgown, robe, and slippers. She should be neat but look fatigued and ill. She wears a loose-fitting cap which completely covers her hair and suggests she is bald.

PLAYING TIME: Ten minutes.

CAST: Angela is about eighteen, a victim of terminal cancer. She has been through the various stages of denial, anger, and grief and has accepted her pending death with grace. She is an inspiration. She shows progressive fatigue as she speaks.

AT RISE: Angela is seated in a large comfortable chair or wheelchair about Center Stage. On the table beside her is a tape recorder. A stuffed toy is on her lap. She holds a microphone.

1   (*As lights focus, ANGELA pulls afghan or blanket over her knees*
2   *and makes herself comfortable. She adjusts and activates the tape*
3   *recorder and speaks into the microphone.*)
4   OK, Mom, Dad, Herbie, Mark. This is Angela and, ummm,
5   it is _____ (*use current date*). If anyone else is listening, this is
6   for you too. Please pay attention. You haven't been very good
7   at listening to me for a while. And, ummm, I know it's hard for
8   you, and you keep telling me, "You're going to be OK. They
9   will find a cure." You are wasting time doing that; you aren't
10   hearing the truth. I'm taping this to make sure I can say
11   something you might listen to. Dad, get someone to type this
12   up, please. I want some of my words to be here, like, after I'm
13   gone.
14   Here, Hoki, give me a hug. (*She hugs stuffed toy.*) Oh, for
15   the benefit of those who haven't met Hoki, he is this silly, gonky
16   turtle (*or other*) Mark gave me. I know he's a toy, but he's a good
17   hugger, and I need all the hugs I can get. You are all good at
18   the hugs. I'm grateful. But back to the subject.
19   I need to say a few things to you when you can't, like,
20   interrupt and contradict me or tell me it's time to rest. (*Long*
21   *pause*) I need to say this, so please listen. (*Pause*) I am going to
22   die. There, I said it. I am dying, as a matter of fact. We all are,
23   of course, but I'm doing it, like, faster than any of the rest of
24   you. You know and I know that there isn't much time left. The
25   doctors have told you that, and you keep denying it. Pretending.
26   Well, I did, too, for a long time. But I was wasting precious
27   living time.
28   I kept saying, like, "This can't happen to me. Why me? I'm
29   too young." I wasted time trying to find someone to blame.
30   Denying the facts. Hiding the truth. I wasted a lot of strength
31   being fighting mad without finding anyone to be mad at. It's
32   not anyone's fault. Remember that. It's not your fault, Mom,
33   Dad. It's not my fault. I didn't do anything to "deserve" this,
34   so I'm not going to take some kind of rap for it.
35   That airhead from Tammy's church who barged in here

1   and tried to get me to, like, examine my life and find out why
2   God is punishing me this way is nauseatingly repulsive. Feel
3   sorry for him and for Tammy. She needs a church which teaches
4   that God loves us. They're only to be pitied for believing all
5   that crap. God didn't make me sick. I am not — was not — some
6   kind of gross sinner. I'm the victim of a kind of natural law or
7   cause and effect or something. I don't know what caused the
8   cancer, but God didn't just decide to pick on me. I don't
9   understand all about God, but I don't believe that's the way he
10 works.
11   Love is the best thing he invented. *(She hugs the toy.)* I
12 appreciate your love and all the prayers and hope. It all helped
13 you accept the, ummm, disappointment. Maybe it helped me
14 that way, too, for I'm the one who's disappointed. Colossally
15 disappointed. I'm disappointed that I am not going to have
16 forty or fifty or sixty more years to taste popcorn and smell
17 gardenias. *(Long pause)* They were super, Mark, the gardenias.
18 Sorry I couldn't make it to the prom. And Dad, the dress was
19 out of sight. I'm not sure I would have chosen that many ruffles,
20 but, well, *(Laughs softly)* you had the right idea. Pale green was
21 right. Thank you, Daddy.
22   I'm disappointed that I won't be here for my eighteenth
23 birthday bash, but it couldn't be as cool as the parties you had
24 for me on the eleventh and twelfth, Mom. Remember the cake
25 with the dinosaur inside? You always come up with something
26 different. You have been, ummm — are — a pretty cool mom.
27 And you, Herbie, are a weird little geek. But I'm glad you get
28 to grow up. Yeah, I am.
29   But I'm un-glad about me. You can't imagine. I guess I'm
30 sorriest that I can't go steady all my life with Mark. No, I'm
31 sorrier that Mark has to, like, go through this alone. After all,
32 in a few weeks I won't have to think about it anymore. He is
33 going to feel it for a long time. I love you, Mark. I really love
34 you, but please go on with life and football and stuff. Don't
35 waste it wondering what it might have been like. *(Wipes her eyes,*

1   *determined not to cry.)*

2   You and I have, like, wasted a lot of time pretending. We

3   both knew I couldn't beat advanced melanoma, but we denied

4   it. We spent a lot of time lying to ourselves instead of enjoying

5   the time we had. Hey, wasn't that canoe trip a blast! We should

6   have done that sooner.

7   I guess the thing that I'm most disappointed about is that

8   I haven't done anything with my eighteen years except a couple

9   of birthday parties and a canoe trip. I haven't composed a song.

10   After all those years of piano lessons, I haven't left something

11   for someone else to play. I haven't written a poem or an essay

12   on how neat life is. Hey, I'm doing the essay right now! Yeah,

13   I am, aren't I? Neat. Pay attention. Copy it. When the tape is

14   worn out, read it. And please listen. Do what you know you do

15   best. If you wait until tomorrow they may find you have multiple

16   sclerosis or AIDS or honkus of the bonkus. Or you could die

17   of pneumonia. Cancer isn't the only thing that does you in.

18   Get up early some morning this week — now — and drive

19   to the beach and buy hot dogs and go barefoot in the sand.

20   Pretend I'm with you, of course. After work some night soon,

21   stop by the halfway house and take one of those thirteen-year-

22   old alcoholics out for a milkshake. Double chocolate. You get

23   vanilla, Herbie, for your zits, you little nerdie nerd. Do

24   something like that for yourself and for me since I can't do it

25   now. I only wish I had done it while I could. *(She shows signs of*

26   *fatigue.)*

27   You wouldn't believe the other things I wish I could do. I

28   wish I could ask Freda Wright to forgive me for spilling egg

29   dye on her Easter dress when we were eight. Remember? She

30   came over to show off her dress, and I even thought about

31   splashing dye on it, but I didn't really mean to do it. Now I

32   don't know where she is. I wish I could tell her how sorry I

33   was — am. I'm really sorry, Freda, if you ever hear this tape.

34   I'd buy you a whole new outfit right now if I could find you.

35   Another thing I wish I could do. I wish I could have, like,

1   a dorm room and a roommate and college banners all over the
2   walls. I wish I could howl my head off for a football team. I
3   wish I could go to college and read Shakespeare. I'd be a real
4   college nerd. Stay up all night and study. Walk in the rain with
5   my guy. Kiss him first. Study. Go bike riding at dawn. *(She*
6   *pauses to shift position. She shows mounting fatigue.)*
7   I'm kinda wiped out right now. I think I will make it to
8   my eighteenth birthday, but that's it. OK, OK, Angie, don't waste
9   the tape feeling sorry for yourself. You've decided not to do
10   that. The worst is over. I have had some time to think about
11   all this. I've known for more than a year that about a year was
12   all I had. Feel sorry for Gary who didn't have a chance to say
13   good-bye when that drunk jerk hit him head-on. He didn't have
14   a hint that his soul was about to sky.
15   Soul. That's really the exciting thing about all this. I've
16   had time to think about things like soul. I don't know how to
17   define it, but I've got it. Soul. All the great philosophers have
18   tried and haven't been able to, like, explain it. I haven't read
19   them all, of course, but I'm on a par with them since I don't
20   know what it is either. *(She manages a laugh.)* I think we just
21   aren't allowed to know. Maybe it is one of those surprises God
22   has for us — finding out there is another dimension to life than
23   eating and breathing and driving cars and dying. I'm looking
24   forward to finding out.
25   I know I have some, like, entity other than this barfy body.
26   Here it is. *(Gestures expansively.)* I am it. My soul is the part of
27   me that isn't sick. I know I have a soul because, I mean, if God
28   makes all this special stuff, he's not going to just dump it. The
29   system, I think, is that bodies and plants grow and blossom
30   and wither and die so that others can take their places and do
31   the same thing over again. That's the plan. But souls don't have
32   to die, and God makes them and keeps them. There is plenty
33   of room for more and more and billions more because they
34   don't take up any space. I mean, I think God collects the souls.
35   You know, like people collect teapots and cars and baseball

1   cards? Well, God collects souls. They're his favorite thing.

2   It will be neat to see what happens — to find out what he

3   does with my soul — to the invisible me. I'm way ahead of you

4   on that. Maybe I will exist in some dimension we can't even

5   fathom. If I can, you better believe I will.

6   And I'm going to find out. Soon. I have to do it alone. I

7   can't take you with me, Mark. Mom. Dad. Herbie. I can't even

8   take this gonky Hoki with me. *(She gives toy a hug.)* I have to — I

9   want to — do this alone. You — you guys — are not ready, but

10   I think I am. I'm not really afraid. Oh, I don't look forward to

11   any more pain, but Dr. Marcher says he will see that it doesn't

12   hurt too much. I think I can take it. So don't worry about me.

13   I worry about you. I don't want you to drag around for several

14   years. I worry a lot more about that than I do about myself.

15   *(She pauses and adjusts pillow and position.)*

16   Tammy was so worried that I would commit suicide. Come

17   on, now, give up early? No way. I want every minute I can get.

18   Life isn't all bad, even when your hair is gone. I still have a

19   brain. Thoughts. Soul. *(Long pause)*

20   One thing I would like. Dad, would you get me some of

21   those roller blades? Wheels. I'd really like some wheels. Yeah.

22   Well, Herbie can, like, break them in for me.

23   Right now I'm washed out, but see, I'm having fun right

24   this minute just talking to you. I've done my essay about life.

25   It is worth it — living — even when you know it won't be for

26   very long. In fact, maybe it's worth more when it's in short

27   supply. I'm not going to miss anything I don't have to.

28   Right now I'm going to hit the sack. Hey, this was a kinda

29   neat idea, making my case and everything. Come on, Hoki, let's

30   take a nap. Check with you later, guys. *(She puts the microphone*

31   *aside, turns off recorder, and settles back on pillow with the stuffed*

32   *toy as lights dim slowly to out.)*

33

34

35

3. CHASTITY

PRODUCTION NOTES

SET: A city street. The performer faces the audience and looks into imaginary windows of shops along the block which the width of the stage represents. Chalked boundaries on the floor indicating position of windows and one entryway into a pawn shop are helpful. No set is necessary, but the director may create a street scene as appropriate.

LIGHTS: Flashing neons, passing headlights of cars, etc., can be simulated to enhance the setting. They should not detract from the performance and are best used as the curtain goes up and as suggested in the script.

SOUND: A police siren; roaring motorcycle passing, stopping, revving up; cruising cars; screeching brakes are effective but not absolutely essential.

PROPS: A carry-all bag decorated whimsically with miscellaneous buttons, old jewelry, and, specifically, a cameo pin. The bag should contain a pair of high-heeled shoes or boots, a small coin purse with coins, and items a teenager would carry.

COSTUME: Chastity wears two layers of clothing important to the revelation of her conflict. The outer garments include winter coat, scarf, fashionable head gear such as man's hat, and running shoes over heavy socks or leg warmers. Beneath the winter clothing she is scantily dressed to suggest a hooker: low-cut top or midriff, miniskirt, black hose. Her hair may be styled in a popular teen mode.

PLAYING TIME: Ten minutes.

CAST: Chastity is a young teenager who has run away from an unhappy home. She is desperate for lodging and food and protection. Her conflict is essentially between her sense of self and her need for shelter. She is a frightened child, desperate human being, and finally, self-respecting, determined young woman.

AT RISE: The stage is empty. Flashing lights, sounds of passing cars, and street noises make a good introduction but should be reduced slowly. Chastity enters, huddled in her winter clothing, hugging herself to keep warm. She walks across the stage facing audience and peering into the invisible shop windows. Pantomime of glass windows and one entryway into a pawn shop should be carefully rehearsed. There should be a strictly delineated space she cannot penetrate with gesture or position. She stops before an imaginary bakery about Down Center.

1   Croissants! Blueberry muffins! Chocolate doughnuts!
2 That's cruel. Painful. How can they do that to all the hungry
3 people on the street — especially me? I'm famished. No. I'm
4 wiped out — majorly starving. *(She digs into her carry-all bag to*
5 *find small purse which contains a few coins.)*
6   Nothing. Well, maybe just enough for one telephone call.
7 Gotta hang onto that in case I have to call home. No. No. I
8 won't. Won't call home. Never. *(She pauses, studying window.*
9 *Sound of distant police siren)*
10   Dad and Mom screaming at each other. Dad takin' off with
11 that skanky woman. I know he did. Mom knew. But she should
12 have done something besides yell. Night after night. *(She is*
13 *angry, hurt.)*
14   At me, too. You'd have thought I was the cat in his life the
15 way she yelled at me. I guess I did break a few rules, staying
16 out late and stuff, but I didn't do Kevin. I didn't, and she kept
17 insulting me. "You and your dad. Ants in your pants." It was
18 a gross thing to say, and I didn't. I didn't. *(She pounds softly on*
19 *the imaginary glass.)*
20   Over and over again, insults. All because she was mad at
21 him or maybe at herself for hitting the vodka and throwing the
22 empties at me. Or did I cause it all? Did I make them hate each
23 other?
24   Well, the goofing off at school was real, of course. I did
25 cut a few classes. But I didn't sleep with anybody. She said I
26 was cheap. She said my hair was a disgrace. All the kids wear
27 frantic hair. That's not such a bad thing to do.
28   And the pot. Of course Kevin had some. And I did try
29 it — so what? No worse than her three martinis every night.
30   She had to find that partly smoked roach, of course. The
31 only time I tried it. The only time.
32   And I'm sorry. Really, I'm sorry, and I said so, but she
33 didn't hear me. Just let me have it with Dad's belt. She'll never
34 do it again because I'll never go home. Never. *(Sound: Autos in*
35 *the distance, brakes)*

1   What kind of weird store is this right here with a bakery
2   and a drug store? Look at all that stuff: ski poles, watches,
3   silver pitchers, jewelry — all in one shop. *(She moves from one*
4   *shop window to another, pantomiming hands against the glass, still*
5   *talking to herself.)*
6   They'll wish they had listened to me a little. What I'm going
7   to do is worse than all the things I did or she imagined I did.
8   I don't really wanna do this. But I gotta eat. *(She pulls her*
9   *coat more tightly around herself and moves on to another "window.")*
10   Quit talking to yourself, Chase. People will think you're
11   flipping out. Maybe I should pretend to be nuts. The police
12   might pick me up and give me a meal.
13   But they'd also wanna know what I'm doing five hundred
14   miles from home. Why I'm walking New York streets in the
15   middle of winter. Yeah, why am I? Because my dad's a cheat
16   and my mom's a bitch who thinks I'm getting laid all the time.
17   Because she doesn't have any faith in me and he teaches me
18   how to cheat.
19   Well, if you don't want to be like him, Chase, what are you
20   doing on a street corner in New York at midnight waitin' for
21   someone to pick you up? Yeah, Chastity Grace Thompson,
22   explain that. *(Long pauses punctuate these speeches as she struggles*
23   *with her conscience.)*
24   Well, I tried every help-wanted sign in New York. "No
25   experience." "Too young." I really tried. *(She walks the full width*
26   *of the stage looking into shop "windows.")*
27   Drugstore. What are all those little boxes with the romantic
28   pictures on them? Oh. Oh yes. I almost forgot. Those I gotta
29   have. Gross! Oh, God, how do I buy condoms without money?
30   I tell the guy to get them?
31   And what do I say to him? How do I tell him he's gotta
32   pay? And how much? And do I have to find a pimp? How do I
33   keep from getting beaten up? What if I get AIDS?
34   How did I get myself into this? How can I do it? Maybe I
35   could find a place to sleep tonight and think it over?

1   But who's going to give me a warm place to sleep? If I
2 wait for a police car to show and then do the come-on? They'd
3 pick me up and take me off to jail — and call Mom and Dad.

4   Except that I won't tell them who I am. I'll make up a
5 name. Can't be Chastity Grace. "Modest. Decent." According
6 to Grandma. She said I would live up to my name. What a laugh.
7 Look at me. Oh, Grandma, I need you now. *(Sound of motorcycle*
8 *approaching, slowing, stopping. She pantomimes watching the rider.)*

9   Oh, not a guy like that. Gross. Oh, no. Huge. Ugly. Dirty.
10 *(She wraps her coat tightly around herself and huddles toward the*
11 *audience as though in the entryway of the pawn shop. Pause, then*
12 *sound of cycle revving up and leaving)*

13   He didn't see me. Oh, he didn't see me. Oh, Grandma, I'm
14 so scared. Talk to me, Grandma. Or just listen. Oh, yes, names.
15 We were talking about names. *(Sound: Police siren as if passing)*

16   Oh God, don't let them see me. Not yet. I don't have to eat
17 tonight. Please! *(She huddles as close to "glass" as possible*
18 *pretending to study contents of window display, her coat pulled around*
19 *her face. She turns slowly.)*

20   Oh that was close. Well, what do I want? What have I got
21 to do? Isn't that what I want? They would feed me and send
22 me home. No. I will not go home. I will not go home. *(She takes*
23 *high heels out of bag and changes shoes then walks to about Center*
24 *Stage and, back to audience as though facing the street, slips off her*
25 *coat revealing her scanty street-walker's garment. She struts the width*
26 *of the stage uncertainly, awkwardly, then turns to face the store*
27 *windows [audience] and sees her own image. Sudden startling self-*
28 *revelation shows on her face. Lights: Soft spot)*

29   No! Oh, no, Chase. That's not you. I can't do this. I can't!
30 *(She wraps the coat and scarf around herself tightly and clutches the*
31 *bag to her chest, snagging her scarf on the cameo. She brings it to her*
32 *cheek.)*

33   Oh, Grandma. Your cameo. Your funny, beautiful, old-
34 fashioned cameo. You said it could take care of me if I ever
35 needed help. Did you mean it would remind me that you trust

1   me to take care of myself? That I'm probably not going to die
2   of hunger? That I'll survive this night some way? That I don't
3   want to be a hooker? But oh, I am hungry. I am so hungry. And
4   I'm freezing. I won't look at the muffins again. I'll look at the
5   skis. I'll keep my coat on. *(She moves to Downstage Left to peer into*
6   *pawn shop window again.)*
7   Skis. Silver pitcher. Silver chains. Look at all the chains.
8   *(She is forcing herself to concentrate.)* Oriental china . . . Lights all
9   on. People in there at this time of night . . . Pawn shop! Loans!
10   Hock shop! That's what this dumb shop is. Money store! All
11   that jewelry! "Qualified customers." Would I be a qualified
12   customer? The cameo! Will they take the cameo? *(She studies it*
13   *carefully.)*
14   Granny, could I come to your house? You never yelled at
15   me. You said a lot of weird things. You said the cameo was the
16   color of innocence and that I was the color of the cameo. You
17   said God made me beautiful. You said God keeps making
18   beautiful people in hopes there will be a perfect one someday.
19   Well, I'm just about to be as ugly as a girl can possibly be,
20   but I'll have one more chance if they'll take this for a while. If
21   they'll lend me some money. *(She unpins the cameo carefully,*
22   *cinches her coat and scarf.)*
23   Granny, I'm sorry I have to hock your beautiful pin, but
24   I'll get it back. And I'll come home to your house. I promise. If
25   they'll just give me enough for a hamburger and a bus ticket.
26   Oh, God, please persuade them to do that. A hamburger and a
27   bus ticket. Please! A hamburger and a bus ticket. *(She takes one*
28   *step forward and reaches for the door at the pawn shop entrance.*
29   *Lights out or quick curtain. Sound: Distant siren)*
30
31
32
33
34
35

4. AURIEL

PRODUCTION NOTES

SET: A physician's examining room. The simplest set will require only a tall reader's stool, but an examining table and other furnishings may be used as the director wishes.

LIGHTS: Interior daylight.

SOUND: No sound effects are necessary.

PROPS: A white cane.

COSTUME: The actor wears a patient's gown over attractive, casual clothing appropriate for a young woman visiting the doctor. Her eyes are heavily bandaged, and she wears large, dark glasses over the bandages.

PLAYING TIME: Eight or nine minutes.

CAST: Auriel is the only character who appears, but she relays the personalities of her brother and parents in what she says. She is in the range of twenty to thirty-five years of age. She is blind — or has been — for most or all of her life and moves about as having lived with that limitation. She has had surgery which could restore her sight, but since she cannot remember having had sight, she is both eager and apprehensive about what vision might be like. She occasionally rocks back and forth gently and doesn't let go of her cane until the last moment before lights out.

AT RISE: Auriel is seated on the reader's stool (or on the end of a doctor's examining table) waiting for the doctor. She shifts position and, leaning on her cane, turns toward Stage Left as if listening for someone to enter.

1   No, not yet, I guess. I wish he would come. I wish this were

2   over. Is it supposed to help for me to sit here alone and wonder?

3   And wait? *(There is a long pause while she tries to occupy herself.*

4   *She taps her cane playfully and swings her feet. She speaks slowly.)*

5   Pink. I wonder what pink is. So many things are pink. It's

6   soft, like my old sweater. It smells like baby powder. Tastes

7   like cotton candy at the fair. That was pink, Mike said, but it

8   wasn't like an old sweater. If color is not to hear, taste, touch,

9   or smell, what is it? *(She rocks slowly, gripping her cane in front of*

10   *her.)*

11   Mom would have come in with me, but I want to do this

12   on my own. I have to prove to them that I can get on with my

13   life whatever happens. I can't depend on them for everything.

14   "Critical medical moment," Dr. Bradley said. Critical

15   everything moment, Dr. Bradley. You are the doctor, but you

16   haven't any idea. And Dr. Kessing said to go ahead and talk to

17   myself. Psychiatric blanket. *(She laughs softly.)* "Talk it out," she

18   said. "You can do it. Whatever happens, you can handle it, a

19   little at a time — just as you always have."

20   But I haven't done this before. Talk to myself. Talk, talk.

21   *(Pause)* When Mike went off to first grade and I had to get to

22   the table alone, I began to realize, I think, that there was more

23   of a difference between us than gender. Mike, where are you?

24   But I told you to stay away. I can't handle everything at once.

25   I'm not ready to see you yet.

26   What is it going to be like to see Mike? I know exactly how

27   much taller he is than I am. I know he's coming when he's a

28   block away. I can feel him kind of hop when he's in a hurry. I

29   know precisely what he's going to say when he opens the door.

30   "Hi, Babe, wanna go for a burger?" Yes, I want to see you, big

31   brother. *(She hugs herself and smiles.)*

32   How different will it be? I know I'll still count steps. How

33   else? But that's easy. The thing that's not easy is understanding.

34   Color. How will I recognize color? Red hot means hot but it

35   doesn't mean red. I know hot. I don't know red. It has to mean

1   whirling and humming like the spinning top Dad gave me when
2   I was little. *(She whirls the stem of her cane in her hands then pushes*
3   *down hard on the hand grip.)*
4   Push down hard and it whirls and whirs and sighs. It was
5   red and green and gold, Dad said. So red must be like humming.
6   Or maybe it tastes like cinnamon. Mom says cinnamon candles
7   are red. If red is like hot, I don't want to get up close, but Dad
8   says you can't feel color or light. *(She covers her face with her*
9   *hands, not letting go of the cane.)*
10   If you can't feel it, what does it mean?! *(She whirls the cane*
11   *between her palms again.)*
12   Talk to yourself, Auriel. Talk.
13   Black is like sleep, they said at school. Black is the opposite
14   of light. It must be like being awake but better. But I know
15   about being awake. How can color be better? How can light
16   be better?
17   Oh, come on, Dr. Bradley. *(She stands, gripping her cane with*
18   *one hand, reaching out with the other, and moves about in a small*
19   *circle, then circles the stool [or examining table] as she talks.)*
20   Let's get this over with. Talking to myself is good for just
21   so long.
22   I do want to know what it is like to see Mom and Dad. But
23   not right now. Not everything at once. What color are they? I
24   know what they are like. Dad is big and gentle and prickly on
25   his chin. He's good at hugging. He has a noisy kiss. There are
26   lines in his face which weren't there when I was little.
27   And Mom looks like love. I know love, and it's Mom. Her
28   voice is a lullaby. She's "No!" and she's "It's OK, Sweetie." She's
29   a promise kept. And she's loneliness when she doesn't come.
30   *(Pause)* But this was my choice. She'll still come when I can't
31   handle it myself. It doesn't make any difference what color she
32   is.
33   It's so confusing. Dr. Bradley says it won't be. He says I
34   will understand quickly. I hope so. I'd like to understand. About
35   transparency, for example. Mike says water is transparent. You

1   can see it but you can see right through it. It has no color. Then
2   he says, "except for the ocean. It's green and blue and even
3   white." So sometimes you can see through it and sometimes
4   you can't? And sometimes it is blue and sometimes green and
5   white (which isn't a color), and that makes it visible? I wonder
6   if even the sighted understand how wonderful that must be. I
7   know the ocean roars and sighs and cools my face. What does
8   it mean to see it? *(She finds the stool [or table] again and sits.)*
9   Oh, come on, Dr. Bradley. These bandages itch. *(She*
10   *scratches the bandages lightly.)* I've been waiting for weeks. Or
11   all my life. Talk, Auriel, talk!
12   I used to think I had a special talent at finding things Mike
13   couldn't find. Like the walnuts dropping on the patio. I could
14   hear them drop, and I'd find them before Mike could. Mom
15   always told me that was remarkable. I wonder if they were just
16   playing games with me. Always made me think I was unusually
17   perceptive.
18   Of course there is just a fifty-fifty chance, Dr. Bradley said.
19   Maybe it won't work. Maybe I won't have to learn everything
20   over again. Maybe I won't be disappointed either way. *(She gets*
21   *up and circles the stool [or table] again, this time using the cane to*
22   *distance herself further but keeping a central position clearly in mind.)*
23   What's the difference between fearing it and hoping for it
24   if you don't know what you are fearing or hoping?
25   "At first just a little light, then a little more, gradually,"
26   he said. But what is light? Dad says a little like gold. And gold
27   is golden curls or King Midas. Which? Gold must be my favorite
28   color, because it is princesses and happiness and comfort and
29   light. And I am Auriel — golden one. But my hair is brown *(or*
30   *other)*, Mom says, so I guess I don't look golden.
31   And I will see my own hair in the mirror. *(She sits suddenly*
32   *and taps her cane on the floor in agitation.)* Oh, really! I'm not sure
33   I can ever understand this or even want to. What's a reflection?!
34   *(She is quiet, rocking gently. Then she sits very still.)*
35   Why am I rationalizing like this? Of course I want to see.

1   I just don't understand.

2   Of course I want it. Stars. I would like to see the stars.

3   Stars are thousands of light years away. Light years? How far

4   is a light year? Years and years distant? But how can anyone

5   see years and years away? You can't see in the dark, but they

6   can see the stars only when it is dark.

7   Do they have any idea what a gift sight must be? *(Pause.*

8   *She is calmer.)*

9   Yes, I want to see the stars. *(The idea seems to help her make*

10   *a decision.)*

11   And God. I would like to see God, but you can't. Nobody

12   can see God, so I guess I'm even there. *(Laughs softly.)* God, I

13   think it will help if you are around in the next few minutes.

14   I've talked to myself about as long as I can, and I can't make

15   any sense of any of it. I could use a little cosmic courage! *(She*

16   *speaks slowly, thinking this through as she speaks.)*

17   I've never seen you, but maybe you can see me. A couple

18   of times in my life I've thought you touched me. Or maybe it

19   was just silence touching. Anyway, it helped. Maybe if I just

20   shut up for a while and listen to your silence I can do this.

21   Thanks for Mom and Dad and Mike and hearing and touching.

22   And if it's OK with you, *(Long pause)* for sight. *(She allows*

23   *the cane to slide to the floor, waits a few seconds, rocking gently, then*

24   *takes off the dark glasses and lifts her face. She is absolutely quiet as*

25   *the lights go out.)*

26

27

28

29

30

31

32

33

34

35

5. CELESTE ESTELLE

PRODUCTION NOTES

SET: The set should reflect the room of an active, intelligent, bouncy, contemporary high school student. At the discretion of the director, either minimal or elaborate furnishings may be used. Elaborate ones would include a single bed, the foot end toward the audience, a bedside table, tape player, and a full-length, freestanding mirror frame without glass placed so that when the actor studies her reflection she is facing the audience Downstage. Minimal furnishings include a small rug and a tape player.

LIGHTS: Interior early evening.

SOUND: Telephone ringing.

PROPS: A telephone with a long cord is essential. Beside the rug (or on a bedside table) is a plate holding a peanut butter sandwich and a long slice of dill pickle, a glass of milk or can of soda, and a banana. One or two stuffed animals or pillows and two or three books are useful. A bedspread is used.

COSTUME: Celeste Estelle, a fourteen-year-old high school freshman, is dressed in brightly colored aerobic exercise clothes. She may wear earrings and bracelets but should not look "punk." She wears no shoes.

PLAYING TIME: Ten minutes.

CAST: Celeste is the only character who appears on stage, but she introduces two friends through telephone conversations. She is an attractive fourteen-year-old whose voice and body express enthusiasm for life.

AT RISE: The curtain opens on an empty room. The telephone is ringing. After two or three rings, Celeste leaps into the room and slides for the phone as if heading into home base on the baseball diamond. She is flat on her stomach as she reaches for the phone. The curled plastic phone cord tangles around her arms and, as she adjusts, even her head.

1   I'll get it! I'll get it! Got it! Hi-eee!

2   Yes, this is Celeste.

3   Meredith, you nerd. "Is this Miss Celeste Gordon?" You

4 know it is.

5   Oh, but I am enthusiastic. I just thought it might be . . .

6   Oh, the rewrite. No, I haven't done it yet. *(She steps over the*

7 *phone cord as if lightly jumping rope.)*

8   I know what he said. "Do it again." Can you register that?

9 Do it all over again? The turkey. "Who Am I? Do I Count?" An

10 essay on personal identity.

11   But I did put the footnotes at the bottom of each page.

12 Like really. I did look up something. I looked up personal

13 identity in the *Readers Guide to Periodical Literature*. And

14 there weren't any articles about me. *(She laughs, swings the phone*

15 *cord around her head.)*

16   But I did find an article: "Identity Crisis. Today's

17 Teenagers." One. I looked up one article. *(She sips her milk or*

18 *soda.)*

19   Oh, pickle. There was lots of "pertinent" . . . how do you

20 like that for being scholarly . . . pertinent information in that

21 article. I don't see why I needed another two. "Three at the

22 minimum." I know he did. Oh, you show-off. Six! You read six

23 articles? No wonder I have to do mine over again. He tells us

24 three sources, and you use six.

25   No. They're out for steak. I'm having pickle and peanut

26 butter. *(She takes a noisy bite of the pickle and then bites into the*

27 *sandwich.)*

28   Peanut butter is nutritious . . . I do too know how to eat.

29 I just bite down and start chewing. *(She does. She talks with her*

30 *mouth full.)*

31   That's because I do have a mouthful of food. I always put

32 food into my mouth when I eat.

33   But my revered parents aren't here to sit down with.

34 They're out stuffing their faces. Totally happy.

35   Those two crocodiles, too.

1   Can you think of a more likely metaphor for my two
2 brothers? I'm not talking about guys. I'm talking about boys —
3 brothers. They are gross juveniles. Weird children.
4   Monty? But he's a guy, a jock. Monty Martin is definitely
5 a guy, a hunk, an awesome hunk.
6   Well, you brought him up.
7   Oh, Meredy, I told you. I told you. He talked to me
8 yesterday for an eon. Well, a couple of minutes. He did. Oh, I
9 can't tell you. He goes . . . it just blows me away to think about
10 it. He goes, "Hi, Celeste." Just like that: "Hi, Celeste." I was
11 totally devastated.
12   Why, I said, "Hi, Monty." Really. I almost pickled.
13   Well, there was an explosion, of course, a maximum
14 explosion of feeling, like, profound, complete understanding.
15 Absolutely max. An actual original collision of galaxies. And a
16 quasar that will last a billion years.
17   A quasar? Like space, you know. A collision of galaxies.
18 Two total galaxies exploding in space. *(She tucks phone over her*
19 *shoulder and slaps two books together to illustrate.)*
20   I am not spacy.
21   No. The quasar is the energy that's left millions of years
22 later. Billions, actually. Visible radiation left over from a head-
23 on out there in space millions and millions and millions of years
24 ago.
25   So I will remember. I'll always remember billions of years
26 from now how Monty went, "Hi, Celeste."
27   I'm not exaggerating.
28   Now? You mean for real? A real collision between
29 galaxies? Sure it could happen. It might solve a lot of problems
30 like doing research to find out who I am. I don't want the world
31 to explode. But you gotta admit it would solve some of our
32 problems.
33   Meredith, you know we do have problems: global
34 warming, pollution, brothers, footnotes.
35   Well, I'm not totally stupid just because I hate footnotes.

1   Astronomy, now ... and space travel. Those awesome rings
2   around Neptune. And pink ice on Triton. Pink ice volcanoes!
3   That I gotta see. And someday ... hey, I gotta get off the phone.
4   Call you back.
5   No, she hasn't said I can't talk to you ... just can't talk
6   more than twenty minutes at one time.
7   I know she's not here, but I do have some personal
8   integrity. Call you back in ten. *(She hangs up the phone and goes*
9   *into an exercise routine, stretching, touching her toes, swinging,*
10   *bouncing. She talks to herself.)*
11   Totally gorgeous I gotta be. This is all for you, Monty
12   Martin. Montgomery M. Martin. "Hi, Celeste." Just like that —
13   "Hi, Celeste." Awesome. *(The telephone rings. She almost strangles*
14   *herself with the phone cord trying to reach it and then holds it next*
15   *to her heart and waits one more ring. She lifts the receiver with care*
16   *and speaks with forced calm.)*
17   Hello.
18   Oh. It's you again.
19   He will too call! I perceive it. But he can't if you hog the
20   phone all night.
21   So don't get pickled. I said I'd call you back. I'll call you
22   back. *(She hangs up the phone again and goes to the mirror facing*
23   *the audience, sizes herself up, brushes her hair several different ways,*
24   *studies the effect, talking to her reflection.)*
25   Well, who are you? I'm Celeste Estelle. That's who I am.
26   Like Dad says, stash that old stuff about finding myself. He
27   says, "I know who you are. You are Celeste Estelle Gordon."
28   Yeah. Celeste Gordon, astronaut. Orbit in space shuttle. Be the
29   first woman on a space station. Wonder how I'll look in a space
30   suit? *(She wraps the bedspread around her head and body and studies*
31   *the effect. She picks up the banana and uses it as a telephone with*
32   *which to rehearse a conversation with Monty.)*
33   Hello. Yes, she is. Just a moment, please. Hello. Who? Oh,
34   yes, Montgomery. This is Celeste Estelle. How nice of you to
35   call ... Oh, no. That won't do. *(She tries a different approach.)*

1   Hi, Monty. No. No. Tomorrow? After school? At my locker?
2   That would be nice ... *(She gives up this angle.)*
3   No, he won't ask me that. He'll ask me to go to Henry's
4   Hangout for a hamburger. Yuk. But I'll go. I'll go, Monty. *(She*
5   *tries again.)*
6   Hello. Who? Oh, hi, Monty. *(The telephone actually rings. She*
7   *drops the banana, leaps to her feet, picks up the phone, and listens*
8   *without saying a word. After a long pause, she barely whispers.)*
9   Hi.
10   Hi.
11   Yes.
12   Yeah.
13   No. Studying. Studying hard. *(She grabs a book.)*
14   History. Civil War. Spanish-American War. Memorizing
15   dates.
16   Me, too. *(Surprised)* Wars and dates. I hate wars and dates.
17   They must have done something else — our ancestors. I mean,
18   besides go to war and underline dates on calendars.
19   Me, too!
20   Oh, I do, too. Pink ice volcanoes on Triton. Little moons
21   like rubies and sapphires in the rings around Neptune.
22   Well, no, but I read a couple of things. And when we get
23   to college ...
24   Oh, Harvard or Vassar or Northwestern.
25   Really? Oh. I'm definitely going to State U, too. Decidedly.
26   Three more years. It seems like eternity.
27   Are you? A paper about quasars? That's what I was going
28   to do! Maybe ... We could do that, I guess. If Mom ... I mean ...
29   We could work at my house.
30   They go on forever and forever and forever eternally.
31   You could never ever learn it all. About space.
32   Me, too, Monty. Me, too. I gotta study, too. Yeah. Bye ... bye,
33   Monty. See ya.
34   See ya.
35   Bye. *(She hangs up the phone, grabs a stuffed animal, hugs it,*

1   *whirls in a circle, Stage Center, pitches the animal onto the bed, and*

2   *makes a statement to the world and to herself.)*

3   That was Monty Martin, Celeste. That was Montgomery

4   Martin sharing his life with Celeste Gordon. He knows what a

5   quasar is and knows who I am and who he is, and he doesn't

6   like wars all hooked together with dates, and we are going to

7   do our homework together. I'm Celeste Estelle Gordon, and I'm

8   fourteen, and I don't have to find out who I am because I already

9   know. I'm going to college someday. And Monty's going to

10   college. Then we'll blast off into space and find out what else

11   is out there. Maybe even green fire or purple people! Ten, nine,

12   eight, here we go, four, three, two, one, lift off! *(She leaps as high*

13   *as she can with "lift off" and lights go out.)*

Jackie Groth as "PRECIOUS"

6. PRECIOUS

PRODUCTION NOTES

SET: Sidewalk. A parking meter stands at about Stage Center as though on the curb. A sign, "Bus Station," may be hung on the backdrop, but no complex staging is necessary. Audience position represents the street.

LIGHTS: Dusk. Street haze.

SOUND: Noise of passing cars or other street sounds may be used before and after Precious speaks, but no background sound is required.

PROPS: Tattered sleeping bag rolled up and tied with rope, large well-worn tote bag of canvas or fabric which contains various personal items including, specifically: cigarettes, mirror, coin purse, coins, toothbrush, small Bible or New Testament, tape measure, bandanna, lipstick, a well-worn envelope, wallet, bottle of pills, address book, pencil, hard bagel, and hypodermic needle.

COSTUME: Precious wears worn jeans, dirty running shoes without socks, two or three body shirts with different necklines, and a severely worn jacket or sweater.

PLAYING TIME: Nine to ten minutes.

CAST: Precious is alone. She is between twenty and forty-five, a street junkie. She is emaciated and dirty. Under stress of withdrawal from various drugs, she exhibits mounting tension and erratic behavior throughout the act.

AT RISE: Precious enters slowly, searching, almost cat-like, for something or someone. Her bedroll is strapped to her back and a tote bag is looped over her shoulder.

1   Where are you, Jerry? Jerry? You said you'd meet me at
2   the bus station. I'm here. Where are you?
3   Talk to yourself, Precious. Don't stop talking. People will
4   stay away from you if you act like a crazy. Stand-up cat. Be a
5   stand-up cat and they'll leave you alone. *(She wanders across*
6   *stage looking into street [audience], alternately cat-like and bold.)*
7   Come on, Jerry. Where are you? I'm trying, Jerry. I'm
8   trying. I need a fix, but I'm going to stop. I'm going to stop.
9   Like you said, I gotta stop. Like you said five years ago.
10   And I did, Jerry. I spent a year in the lock-up because
11   they figured I was hustling. I wasn't. There is an easier way
12   for a woman to make money. Lots of easier ways to get the
13   good stuff.
14   But I really want to go straight. Taste an orange. You gotta
15   help if I'm goin' to make it this time. I'm going to make it. Make
16   it. Make it.
17   I need something to hang onto until you get here. I need
18   something . . . *(She sees the parking meter and hurries to it, grabs it*
19   *possessively.)*
20   Ah, a money post. A tree. I can hang onto this tree. *(She*
21   *slides to the floor against the meter, still embracing it.)*
22   A tree you gotta pay for. OK, I'll pay for my tree. My space.
23   I got money. Money is easy to get. Just hard to keep. But I can
24   pay for my tree — my space. This is mine, and I'm goin' to stay
25   right here until Jerry comes.
26   Money. Where's my money? *(She takes off the bedroll and*
27   *hooks the straps over the meter post. She begins taking items out of*
28   *her tote bag, examining them carefully at first and laying them around*
29   *herself in a circle.)*
30   Where's my money? Cigarettes. I have a right to a cigarette.
31   Here's my cigarettes. Toothbrush. Gotta take care of my teeth.
32   Gotta have good teeth. Little Bible. Read about how Jesus
33   treated the woman they wanted to stone. Jerry, he was good
34   to her. Don't you forget me. *(She continues to remove items from*
35   *her bag and places them in a circle around herself on the sidewalk.)*

1   Tape measure. Measure my space. Keep people out of my
2   space. Mirror. Don't look right now. Don't ever look after a bad
3   trip. Bad trip. That last fix was cut. I know it was. I was burned.
4   I'll kill that tout. "Good stuff," he said. "Good stuff." And I
5   freaked out.

6   Keep talking, Precious. Only keep it down. No use to tell
7   these street people your problem. Poor street people. Hurry,
8   Jerry. It's been eight hours. I wanna quit, but you just don't
9   know.

10   My legs feel like somebody's beatin' on them, like, with a
11   hammer. *(She rubs her legs, then her arms, then her face. She is in*
12   *pain. She searches her bag, finds a bandanna, and wipes her eyes and*
13   *nose.)*

14   Nose running like a faucet. Jerry, I gotta have a fix if you
15   don't get here. No. I gotta stay put. Parked. *(She hugs the meter*
16   *post and looks up at the timer.)*

17   Uh-oh. Money post. Money tree. Where's my money? I'm
18   going to pay for this spot and stay here until Jerry comes. I
19   gotta right to a space. This money tree is public property, so
20   I'm public. I put in my money and I'm entitled to stay. *(She finds*
21   *a small coin purse, empties it out on the sidewalk. She counts coins.)*

22   Five cents. A dime. A quarter. *(Studies the meter.)* "Fifteen
23   minutes for a nickel. Fifteen minutes for a dime. Fifteen minutes
24   for a quarter." Now which? Choices? Do I wanna spend a nickel
25   or a quarter or a dime for fifteen minutes of space? Time. Why
26   don't they make up their minds? Bus station meter. Place where
27   you have to wait, so they charge you for waiting. Baby, that
28   makes sense. I'm gonna be sick. I don't even know where to
29   get a fix in this town. I don't see no wire anywhere. I know a
30   wire when I see one. They find you. They know you need it. No
31   wire. No wire.

32   Just a snort of something would help. Or cough syrup.
33   Oh, Yeah, I gotta cough. *(She fakes a cough.)* Drug store? No, I
34   gotta stay here.

35   Pay the money tree, Precious. Remember, pay the money

1   **tree before some cop comes.** *(She finally puts a coin in the meter*
2   *and slides back down to a sitting position.)*
3   **There. My space. I paid for my space. Gotta right . . .** *(She*
4   *wipes her eyes and nose again with bandanna and removes her sweater.*
5   *She is sweating.)*
6   **Hot. Allergy. Yeah, it's allergy makes my eyes water.** *(She*
7   *laughs.)* **Allergy. I also gotta go to the ladies' room. No, I gotta**
8   **keep my space. I paid for this space. Hurry up, Jerry.** *(She hugs*
9   *her middle.)*
10   **Jerry, baby, you are sweet, and I am gonna hate you for**
11   **helpin' me. I already hate you. I need a fix so bad. Need a high.**
12   **Need a nod. You gotta help me.** *(She is increasingly agitated,*
13   *twisting, tapping her feet. After a pause, she stands up as if to leave*
14   *then, during the following speech, takes the rope off her bedroll and*
15   *ties herself to the meter post, knotting it securely several times.)*
16   **I'm gonna stay right here. I paid. My money tree. Stay,**
17   **Precious. Play it cool, Precious. You are not going to be sick.**
18   **You are not going anywhere. You don't need the ladies' room.**
19   **You are staying right here. You don't need a fix.** *(She slides to*
20   *the sidewalk, her legs stretched out in front of her, her body secured*
21   *to the post. One at a time her legs begin to jerk, relax, and jerk. During*
22   *the next speech she is experiencing involuntary spasms of kicking*
23   *motion of her legs, a symptom of withdrawal.)*
24   **Here it comes. Jesus, I need a fix. I'm gonna up-blast. No,**
25   **Precious, you are going to stay cool. You are not going to vomit.**
26   **You are going to wait for Jerry. Chill out.**
27   **Jerry, how did you do it? How did you go straight? You**
28   **bastard, you gave me the first sniff, and then the joint. I was**
29   **just a chippie. Then lotsa joints. Then the coke. Then heroin.**
30   **Drug of the sophisticates, you said. Oh, yeah, sophisticates.**
31   **Look at me. Precious the sophisticate.** *(She searches her bag and*
32   *brings out a hypodermic needle, studies it, and rubs it on her face and*
33   *forehead. She rolls up her sleeve and rolls it back and forth on her arm.)*
34   **Are you really clean, Jerry? Got a real job? Pay checks?**
35   **A pad? I don't believe it, but that's what you said.**

1   Keep talking, Precious. Remember, you are going straight.
2   Get a job. Get a paycheck. Taste some oranges. Cigarettes.
3   Have I got a cigarette? Smoke. Where's my cigarettes? *(She*
4   *searches her bag and then the belongings around her on the sidewalk.)*
5   How did this stuff get out here? Put it back, Precious.
6   Clean up your act. Put your junk back into your purse. *(She*
7   *begins to put things back into her bag. Her legs continue to jerk. She*
8   *is in pain.)*
9   Don't try to stand up. Put the stuff back. *(She returns some*
10   *items to bag, takes others out, finds her cigarettes, and begins to look*
11   *for a lighter.)*
12   Lighter. Where's my lighter? Can't smoke without lighting
13   the cigarette. Lighter, lighter, find your lighter.
14   Ah, here it is. *(She puts the cigarette into her mouth without*
15   *lighting it and snaps the lighter on and off. She does not smoke. She*
16   *confuses the cigarette with the needle, putting the needle and then the*
17   *cigarette into her mouth. She does not speak for a long moment. Then*
18   *her legs begin jerking violently.)*
19   Oh, God, it hurts. *(She doubles over, holding body in a strong*
20   *self-hug.)*
21   Don't yell, Precious. Hold on. Hold on. Jesus! God! *(She*
22   *drops cigarette and rocks back and forth, still holding the hypodermic*
23   *needle and rolling it back and forth on her face.)*
24   Shut up, Precious. Some cop will hear you and take you
25   in. Jerry'll never find you. Shut up. Shut up. *(She hugs herself*
26   *again.)*
27   God it hurts. I gotta have a fix. I gotta. *(Her legs jerk violently.*
28   *She tries to untie the knot in the rope.)*
29   How did I do that? I tied that knot. I can untie it. I gotta
30   untie it. *(She frantically tries to untie the knot but fails.)*
31   Jerry, hurry! Untie me! Get me outta this. Jerry, where
32   are you? Bring a fix with you, and hurry. I can't even get to the
33   ladies'. You maniac, don't do this to me! Where are you, Jerry?
34   You promised. You promised. You piss head! *(Showing pain in*
35   *legs, arms, head, as she does it, she tries to put belongings back into*

1   *her bag and names them, taking deep breaths after each item. Her*
2   *legs continue to jerk. She continues to hold tightly to needle.)*
3   **Cigarettes. Mirror. Comb. Lipstick. Letter from Jerry.**
4   **Coin purse. Wallet. Address book. Measuring tape. Bagel. Hard**
5   **bagel. Bandanna. Valium.** *(She focuses on the valium bottle then*
6   *opens it and scatters the pills in one sudden gesture. Still holding*
7   *needle, she dries her forehead, neck, and face with bandanna. She*
8   *clearly is in agony.)*
9   **Jerry, it hurts. It hurts like hell. I'm not gonna scream.**
10   **They'll throw me in the lock-up again. Hurry, Jerry. Jesus, it**
11   **hurts. Yeah, I tied myself to the post. I tied myself good.**
12   **I'm gonna go straight if it kills me. I'm gonna go straight.**
13   **Jerry, you're gonna come around that corner, and you're**
14   **gonna be clean. You're gonna walk over here and say, "Hi,**
15   **Babe!" And you're gonna lift me up.** *(She rises slowly, hanging*
16   *onto meter post.)*
17   **And untie me for good.** *(She is standing.)*
18   **And I'm gonna go clean.** *(She holds up needle, clearly visible,*
19   *studies it, and in one calculated move, drops it to sidewalk and crushes*
20   *it with her foot.)*
21   **Clean!** *(Lights go out.)*
22
23
24
25
26
27
28
29
30
31
32
33
34
35

7. MAMIE

PRODUCTION NOTES

SET: The act takes place on a city sidewalk, in a mall, or at the entry of a large department store. A bench is useful, but no scenery is necessary.

LIGHTS: Daylight, exterior.

SOUND: Subdued street noises may be used as the actor enters and leaves, but the performance may be done without background sound.

PROPS: The performer pushes a baby stroller in which a large doll is seated. The doll is fully dressed in real baby clothes — not the usual new doll finery. It should look as much like a real baby as possible. A blanket is used in the stroller, but it should not substitute for baby clothing or hide the doll which should be clearly visible to the audience. A baby bottle and stuffed toy and rattle are tucked in beside the doll.

COSTUME: Mamie's clothing lacks coordination. For example, she might wear a dress over long pants or a summer top and an Alpine cap. Her hair is disheveled and unstyled. Her costume reflects mental disorganization but not poverty.

PLAYING TIME: Ten minutes or less.

CAST: Mamie is the only character who appears on stage, but the doll takes on real personality because of the way she handles it and talks to it. Mamie is about forty, the victim of a tragedy and unable to face reality. She lives in a world that might have been.

AT RISE: The stage is empty. Mamie enters and proceeds to about Center Stage pushing the stroller. Her uncoordinated gait is something between a shuffle and a stroll.

1   *(MAMIE is mumbling almost inaudibly as she enters.)*

2   **Nonnie. Nonnie. Me and Nonnie. Nonnie. Nonnie.** *(At about*

3   *Center Stage she turns slightly toward the audience as if passing a*

4   *shop window. She pauses and observes the display. There is a distinct*

5   *contrast in voice and manner when she speaks.)*

6   **Well, look at that, Nonnie. Dolls and teddy bears out**

7   **already, and it's only October. Dolls and teddy bears, make-**

8   **believe babies. Make-believe people. They would have us buy**

9   **make-believe babies for our babies to love. Would you like a**

10   **make-believe baby for Christmas, Nonnie?** *(She strolls on, talking*

11   *to the doll, turning and retracing her steps as she speaks.)*

12   **I feel sorry for people who don't have real babies. College**

13   **girls with their teddy bears. That Brenilda across the park with**

14   **her poodles. Walks them every day. And talks to them. Dogs.**

15   **Poodle taking the place of a baby. Silly, silly woman. Doesn't**

16   **know what she's missing. Or Cresence who talks to her plants.**

17   **Says they're easier to look after than babies. No diapers to**

18   **change. Irrational. Absolutely irrational.** *(She faces another*

19   *display and picks up the doll. Her tone again becomes monotonous.)*

20   **Nonnie. Nonnie. Nonnie? You've been so good all morning.**

21   **Are you going to cry? Is someone hurting you? Did that doctor**

22   **hurt you, Nonnie?** *(She puts the doll over her shoulder as if to "burp"*

23   *it.)*

24   **Tummy ache? There, there. Don't cry. You are OK. You're**

25   **not cold, are you? You must not get cold.** *(She takes a blanket*

26   *from the stroller and throws it around the doll, comforting it, rocking*

27   *it next to her chest.)*

28   **Here's your banky. Banky. Banky for Nonnie. Nonnie**

29   **loves his banky. Dragging it around the house with you. That's**

30   **better. You are always so good when we go out. Never complain.**

31   **Never cry. Such a good boy. Good baby, Nonnie. Nonnie.**

32   **You must not get cold. Must not cough. No. Doctor Chester**

33   **was so wrong. He said your cough was serious. Said you should**

34   **go to the hospital and have oxygen. But I know what he really**

35   **wanted. He really wanted a good baby like you for his own.**

1 He would have taken you home with him. He couldn't fool me.
2 Doctors can do that — take babies from the hospitals when
3 they want to. Do you know how many babies disappear from
4 hospitals? Doctors. Doctors do it. *(She pantomimes responding to*
5 *someone going by.)*
6   Why do people always look at us like that? Hasn't she ever
7 seen a good baby? I heard what she said. "It's a doll!" she said.
8 Well, of course. Nonnie, you are so perfect people think you
9 are a doll. Perfect baby. Real doll. *(She pantomimes watching*
10 *others pass.)*
11   I won't let them hurt you, Nonnie. When the doctor saw
12 how quiet you were he couldn't believe it. "He's not coughing
13 anymore," he said. Of course not. You were fine. You were
14 asleep. And he didn't get to steal you from the hospital. He
15 would have. Doctors do that. But I just held you until you quit
16 coughing.
17   And then they made me go to a hospital. And they checked
18 everything. Nothing wrong. No pneumonia. Some little thing
19 they said I couldn't pronounce. But I can pronounce any of
20 their silly terms. Schizophrenia. Paranoia. Psychosis. And I
21 know what they mean, too. But that doctor didn't tell me I had
22 any of them. They have to tell you what it is if you're sick. He
23 didn't tell me anything. I'm fine. Look at me. Do I look sick?
24 He just wanted to keep me in the hospital and away from you.
25 But they couldn't do that. Here I am. I'm a good mother. I'm
26 strong and healthy. I take good care of you. Take a pill, they
27 said. Take your medicine regularly. You'll be fine.
28   And when I came home — there you were, waiting. Quiet
29 and clean. No cough. In your little chair. Sweet and quiet. I
30 didn't have pneumonia. I was fine. I don't need any medicine.
31 Wash it down the toilet. Wash it down. Wash it down. Down.
32 Down. Down. *(She laughs at her own word play, then sits on the*
33 *bench and holds the doll. She takes the rattle from the stroller and*
34 *positions the doll's hand over the rattle.)*
35   So quiet and good you won't even use a rattle. Here, try

1   it, Nonnie. Try making a little noise with a rattle. You don't
2   have to be absolutely quiet now. Try the rattle. *(She holds doll's*
3   *hand over the rattle and shakes it furiously.)*
4   There! That's the way. Shake it hard, Nonnie. Hard! Good.
5   See, you can make noise. Shake it harder, Nonnie. Harder!
6   Louder! Noise! Make a noise! Rattle! Rattle! Rattle! *(This is a*
7   *violent moment. She stands, throws the bottle and the stuffed toy, and*
8   *finally, the rattle, kicking them in fury. Then she stops suddenly, turns*
9   *toward audience, and stands absolutely still for a long moment. In*
10   *the next speech she is calm and quiet. Holding doll on her hip, she*
11   *begins to rock slowly back and forth.)*
12   Look at that. Rocking horses. Rocking, rocking, rocking.
13   Would you like one for your birthday next spring? You'll be
14   five. No two. You'll be two. Your dad says you'll be twenty. He
15   thinks you are grown, but look at you. You're not quite two.
16   He's joking. He's confused. He wants you grown up so you can
17   go fishing with him. So you can cut the grass. Take out the
18   garbage. I like you the way you are — not quite two. Wonderful
19   two. *(She gently places the doll in the stroller and pushes it back and*
20   *forth in a rocking motion.)*
21   He looks so old, your dad. He worries. He looks forty-five.
22   I will be twenty-five my next birthday. And he's two years older
23   than I am, your dad. Does that make him forty-five? But I'm
24   twenty-five. Thirty-five? He gets mixed up. How can you be
25   twenty when you are still a baby? I was twenty when you were
26   born? Oh, it doesn't matter. I hate math. You're going to be two
27   on your birthday.
28   Remember last year's party? You were two last year. Two
29   is the best time. All your parties have been two parties.
30   Remember when I got you a tricycle? You just weren't ready
31   for it. After a couple of years your dad gave it away. He's not
32   very patient.
33   No reason to hurry. You'll grow up soon enough. And
34   you are always so good. You never cry. Never cry.
35   And you never cough. That silly doctor. You could die, he

1   said. And we just showed him. I knew what to do when you
2   were sick. I kept you warm and held you all night. Your favorite
3   rocking chair. Your blanket. I held you all night. All night. You
4   quit coughing. You were such a good boy. Quit coughing.
5   Absolutely quiet. Didn't even cry.

6   And now you are almost two and never cough. That doctor
7   moved away years ago. If he could see you now, almost two
8   and a perfect doll.

9   Perfect, quiet baby. Never sick. Never cry. Never cough.
10 **Perfect doll.** *(She pushes the stroller Off-stage, her gait the same as*
11 *upon entrance. Her tone returns to the original monotone.)*

12   Nonnie. Nonnie. Nonnie. Me and Nonnie. Nonnie, Nonnie.
13 *(Lights out)*

8. MARY BELLE CANTO

PRODUCTION NOTES

SET: Seaside at the beach. No scenery is required but can be suggested by scattered shells and driftwood.

LIGHTS: Early morning daylight.

SOUND: Background sound of waves washing the shore regularly may be used to introduce the act but must be diminished slowly as the actor appears and eliminated during her speech. If used, this sound should be repeated at the end of the scene. Off-stage piano accompaniment may be used for vocal exercise and solo.

PROPS: The performer wears a lightweight backpack containing a filled plastic water bottle.

COSTUME: Actor wears jogging outfit. It should be clean and bright but may suggest wear.

PLAYING TIME: Ten minutes. Time may vary according to length of vocal solo.

CAST: Mary Belle Canto* may be anywhere between twenty and forty-five. She must have a fine singing voice. She is cheerful, hopeful, and enthusiastic about life. She appreciates the mystery of the cosmos.

AT RISE: The stage is empty. Mary Belle runs on, exhausted from jogging, laughing as if in response to the sea. She faces audience about Center Stage.

* *bel canto: a quality of singing which exhibits purity of tone and precise vocal technique.*

1   Whoo! *(Out of breath)* **Good morning sea! Good morning**
2   **wind! Good morning whales and sharks and all you creatures**
3   **out there in the deep, deep blue!** *(She drops to the "sand," removes*
4   *shoes, and takes a drink of water from her water bottle in the backpack.)*
5   **What a morning. What a beautiful morning. Listen to the**
6   **waves. Listen to the laughter — of the universe.**
7   **Hey, that was poetic, wasn't it?! Maybe it is God's**
8   **laughter — the sea. Some poets hear sobs, but listen to that!**
9   **Ha, ha, *ha!* Ha, ha, *ha!* Laughter for sure. Or maybe a song.**
10   **We ought to pay attention to it — to find out what it is. We**
11   **should eavesdrop on the cries and conversations and songs of**
12   **the cosmos.** *(She pantomimes working feet into the sand.)*
13   **Oooh — does that feel good. Even the sand has a message:**
14   **Everything has a purpose. Sand? Foot massage superb.**
15   **Paradise for tired feet. Why do we punish our feet by making**
16   **them run on sidewalks when we could walk in the sand?**
17   **Oh, I know, of course. Ms. Miriam says, "Run, run, run.**
18   **Breathe. Breathe. Breathe from your toes." But it's the**
19   **diaphragm she's thinking about. Run. Force yourself to**
20   **breathe. And the poor toes have to do the work. I didn't see**
21   **her jogging thirty blocks to the beach this morning.** *(She rises*
22   *and does some cool-down routines.)*
23   **But she wants me to stay in shape and to sing. She's right.**
24   **I'm doing it. I'm doing aerobics. I'm running. I'm breathing**
25   **from the toes! I'm singing, and that's what I'm supposed to do.**
26   **Are you listening, little fishes of the sea? Little octopi, little**
27   **starfish. Come on, now, talk back to me.** *(She takes deep breaths*
28   *and then explores her vocal range with a slow a capella warmup. This*
29   *routine is paced carefully and timed as if in response to the rhythm*
30   *of waves. The actor "conducts" with an imaginary baton. Either a*
31   *special scale routine or the traditional "do re me" exercise may be used.*
32   *She pauses and "directs" after each syllable or as appropriate to her*
33   *selection.)*
34   **Do.** *(Swings baton.)* **Re.** *(Swings baton.)* **Me . . . Fa . . . Sol . . .**
35   **La . . . Ti . . . Do!**

1 Perfect! The best scale exercise I've done since yesterday.
2 Your rhythm and tone are faultless — on the button. Perfect
3 antiphon. Ms. Miriam would be pleased. *(She pauses and strolls,*
4 *exercising toes and kicking up "sand," then faces audience again,*
5 *directing comments skyward.)*
6 Hello, majestic Creator. Mysterious architect of the soul.
7 Do you actually hear one little earth creature like me? I hope
8 so, because I want to thank you. Thanks for this splendid
9 morning. Thanks for the sea, for its rhythm. Thanks for my
10 healthy lungs. I'm grateful that I can run. And sing. Thanks
11 for my voice. I'd like to believe you blessed me with it for some
12 purpose. Of course you gave whales singing voices too. What
13 incredible coloraturas! They don't sing on stage, but they sing
14 for each other. Is that what you had in mind?
15 Anyway, thanks for all this. I have so much, I feel guilty
16 about asking for more, but I really need a job. Could you help
17 me out on that? In society the way we've worked it out, we
18 have to have money to exchange for food. Bus fare. Shoes. I'm
19 down to one pair of running shoes and one pair of not-quite-
20 worn-out pumps for auditions. They don't understand at
21 auditions about walking barefoot. I really need a job that pays
22 money. Dollar bills. You know, signed checks. I have to pay
23 the landlord. He won't take a song. Ms. Miriam needs money
24 for her orange juice and shoes, too. It's fair. It's fair for me to
25 pay her so that she can eat. But right now no one seems ready
26 to pay me for what I do. No one seems to need sopranos. Or
27 actors. Or writers.
28 There's a real hang-up about paying creators. It seems as
29 if creating would be high priority since that's what you do, but
30 not much money in it. God, that is what you do — create, right?
31 And we accept your endless works of art without so much as
32 a nod. Pink and gold sunsets. Sky-skimming redwoods.
33 Smashing waves. Little-bitty turtles and violets. That may
34 explain why our creative efforts are not highly valued. The
35 artist is supposed to enjoy his work so much he wants to give

1   and give the way you do. Oh, I like to sing, of course, and people
2   ask me to, but they always seem surprised when they learn I
3   need to eat.

4   So I'm trying to remember to thank you — even if others
5   don't — for all this. *(Gestures to sea and sky.)* For whales and
6   minnows and hot coffee and sand for tired feet. Thank you for
7   violins and pianos. For parents and gifted teachers. And sea
8   gulls.

9   Did you see the sea gulls lined up listening to me when I
10   practiced yesterday? I thought I was alone when I sang out
11   here — no critics — and then I turned around, and there they
12   were — a gallery of sea gulls, patient and polite, just waiting
13   to see what strange thing I would do next. *(Laughter)* It was
14   funny but wonderful. Sea gulls for an audience.

15   Thanks for the gulls. And the whales. Thanks for giving
16   whales an operatic range to rival Pavarotti's. It would be fun
17   if we could get close enough for a chorus, but I'm sure you
18   know why you gave them the sea for their song and me the
19   open sky for mine. Thanks for the whales and the waves and
20   the depths of sea and sound — profound, mysterious sound.

21   And for my voice. I have it, so you must have given it to
22   me. Was it an accident of genes, or did you really mean it as a
23   gift? I'm not very good at waiting tables, tending bar, or coping
24   with computers. I think you must have given me a good voice
25   for a purpose. Singing is what I do best.

26   But it would be helpful if your other-than-singing
27   creatures saw some value in my making pleasant noises with
28   my natural equipment. *(Laughter)* For I have to eat, too. As I
29   explained, our system requires that I pay for food. And rent.

30   No, I'm really not discouraged. I'm quite accustomed to
31   wondering where the rent money is coming from. Something
32   has to happen soon. Thanks for my friends who help sometimes.
33   And for tax refunds. And coupons. And relatives who believe
34   in me. It is a good system when it works.

35   Could you take a song as a way of saying thanks for all

1   **the things you hand out? For hope. For dreams of audiences**
2   **giving me standing ovations?** *(She curtsies.)* **For the sea and the**
3   **gulls and the sand?** *(She sings a hymn of praise. Choose a song*
4   *appropriate to the voice and singing style of the performer. Possible*
5   *choices include "Mine Eyes Have Seen the Glory" [melody: "Battle*
6   *Hymn of the Republic"] by Julia Ward Howe, "Christ From Whom*
7   *All Blessings Flow" by Charles Wesley, or "All Praise to Thee, My*
8   *God, This Night" by Thomas Ken. These popular hymns may be found*
9   *in most church hymnals. Another choice may be the popular gospel*
10 *number, "How Great Thou Art," available from Manna Music Inc.,*
11 *P.O. Box 218, Pacific City, Oregon, 97135. (503) 965-6112. The*
12 *performer must remember that the entire act is a unit, this song being*
13 *a part of the total impression. She is a grateful and prayerful artist*
14 *at the seashore singing to God. When the song is finished, she takes*
15 *a bow to the "sea.")*
16   **Oh, thank you, God, and my friends — dolphins,**
17 **swordfish, eels and crab and flounder. Thank you for your**
18 **rhythm and grace and tolerance of me and of all of us who**
19 **walk instead of swim. I can hear your applause in the currents.**
20 **I can't do an encore right now, though, for this system in which**
21 **I'm involved requires that I get home and put on the pumps**
22 **and try once more for a job. It has to be there somewhere.**
23   **See you tomorrow. If I get that job parking cars I can still**
24 **come in the morning hours. Wish me luck.** *(Actor exits running*
25 *and waving at the "sea.")*
26
27
28
29
30
31
32
33
34
35

9. HARRIET HATTERBY

PRODUCTION NOTES

SET: An exclusive hat shop. A hat tree fully supplied with a variety of women's hats stands slightly Right of Center. A small table or chair is useful. The performer pantomimes the use of a large, full-length mirror Center Stage.

LIGHTS: Indoor, afternoon.

SOUND: No background sound is required.

PROPS: Numerous women's hats. Several specifically shaped and styled hats are necessary: baseball cap, merry widow hat, pillbox, pirate hat, cloche, bonnet, turban, beret, sailor straw or bowler, picture hat or beach hat. See script for descriptions.* Hand mirror.

COSTUME: Harriet Hatterby is impeccably dressed in an unembellished black dress or suit and high heels. The costume must be fashionable but understated so that nothing detracts from attention to the hats and the performer. The incongruity of hats and her smart clothing is important for comic contrast. She carries a simple black bag.

PLAYING TIME: Variable. Act is designed for flexibility in use of specific hats. A particular hat and lines related to it may be eliminated, reducing performance time. If all hats are used, playing time is eleven minutes.

CAST: Harriet, the only performer who appears, is more stand-up comic than player of a role. She could be between twenty-five and sixty-five; her age is not as important as her sense of the entertaining differences among human beings . . . and hats. Designed to be ridiculous, the act is a comic skit rather than a play. It is fast-paced and snappy.

AT RISE: Harriet enters from Left and walks directly to the hat rack.

* *Specifics about most of the hats are the courtesy of* The Hat, Trends and Traditions, *Madeleine Ginsburg, Barron's, N.Y., 1990.*

1   **Oh, here we are. Hats. Hats. Hats. Lovely, lovely.** *(She walks*

2 *around the rack several times, almost dancing in her excitement.)*

3   **Choices. Oh, look at the choices. An abundance of hats.**

4 **A plethora of hats!** *(She raises her voice as if talking to the clerk or*

5 *proprietor and pitches her bag on the chair or table.)*

6 **Oh, Clarisse. You have scores of new hats. Do you have one of**

7 **those cute new ones like a baseball cap? I think that's a darling**

8 **style.** *(She finds the cap herself. It has a baseball cap shape, but is*

9 *either felt or silk, definitely faddish.)*

10   **Here's one. Oh, cute! Clever. Ingenious.** *(She puts it on, tries*

11 *it at several angles, observing herself in an imaginary mirror Center*

12 *Stage. She faces audience and pantomimes this mirror with precision.*

13 *She sings.)*

14   **Take me out to the ball game! Let me wear a cute cap!**

15 *(Speaks.)* **Look at this, Clarisse! Isn't this just the cleverest?** *(She*

16 *swings an imaginary bat.)*

17   **One, two, three, and you're out at the old ball game. Why**

18 **didn't someone think of this before? I love it. Casey will be so**

19 **impressed. I'll take it. I'll take two. No, wait. What is this?** *(She*

20 *returns cap to rack and chooses a merry widow hat of contemporary*

21 *design, an elaborate hat with a large crown and brim flamboyantly*

22 *decorated with feathers and plumes.)*

23   **Now, Hattie Hatterby, here's a hat for you. Don't you think**

24 **so, Clarisse? London, here I come! All I need is a bustle** *(She*

25 *pantomimes)* **and a parasol, maybe.** *(She struts across the stage in*

26 *the manner of a great lady of 1910.)*

27   **This could be for me — if I could carry it. And if it were**

28 **1910. A bit burdensome.** *(Returns hat to rack.)* **Like wearing a**

29 **cocktail table on your head. Let's see. What's this? Small**

30 **enough.** *(She returns the merry widow to the rack and chooses the*

31 *pillbox hat — a small, round brimless hat with flat crown and straight*

32 *sides. She tries it at several angles.)*

33   **Where does one wear one of these — down a narrow aisle**

34 **in the canned fruit section? Who am I in a pillbox? A bellboy?**

35 *(Pantomimes opening a door and bowing.)* **I'm amazed that these**

1 are coming back. Forties? Fifties? They must have been short
2 on material and imagination. What a lack of predication. No
3 declaration. Dull. Not for me. *(She exchanges the hat for a*
4 *fashionable "pirate" hat. It can be in felt or straw and has a round*
5 *crown and about a four-inch brim which is turned up in front and*
6 *anchored with a silk rose. It may also be trimmed with cord and tassel.)*

7   **What's this?** *(She tries it with rose in back, then front. She*
8 *pantomimes before mirror.)*

9   **Where does the flower go, Clarisse, front or back? Oh.**
10 **Front. It's a pirate hat! Heave, ho, a marauding go! This must**
11 **be the neo-romantic look. Is the rose for tossing into the drink**
12 **after the victim walks the gang plank? And where's the dagger?**
13 **I'd have to wear a dagger in my belt, wouldn't I?**

14   **And a ship. This hat requires a ship — the Jolly Roger or**
15 **Happy Harvey or some such. What do you think, am I the pirate**
16 **type? A purloiner, pilferer? Am I a lady buccaneer? Paula**
17 **Jones? Or old Captain Kidder?**

18   **No, I don't think so. I faint at the sight of blood. I'm more**
19 **apt to heave than to ho. No pirate hat for me, rose or no rose.**
20 *(She returns the hat to rack and selects a cloche, a hat typical of the*
21 *twenties — tight-fitting and pulled low over the forehead. She can*
22 *barely see out and pantomimes appropriately, stepping gingerly with*
23 *arms stretched out before her.)*

24   **Clarisse, do you sell seeing-eye dogs to go with this one?**
25 **Or a cane? I can't see out.** *(She picks up the hand mirror and holds*
26 *it to her face.)*

27   **I'm in here somewhere. Maybe if I put it on upside down.**
28 *(Turns the hat but still can't see.)* **This is the silliest thing I ever**
29 **saw. Maybe flappers didn't have to see to do the Charleston.**
30 *(She does a quick Charleston step.)*

31   **I know. It's designed for the woman who's just had a face**
32 **lift. No one will recognize her for about three weeks. Then,**
33 **voilà!** *(Grabs it at the crown and removes it.)* **New face! New me!**
34 **But not for me. I'll face up to things the way I am. This one is**
35 **not for me.** *(She returns the cloche to rack and chooses a bonnet. It*

1 *is a contemporary version of the bonnet which fits the back of the head*
2 *and has a funnel-shaped brim to shade the face. It is decorated with*
3 *ribbons and bows.)*
4   Oh, westward, ho! Isn't this just too cunning? A bonnet.
5 Now is that supposed to be for a baby or a grandmother? To
6 wear in a covered wagon or a Porsche? *(She pantomimes driving*
7 *horses.)*
8   Whoa, Noah! Whoa, Bess! Covered wagon, for sure. I'd
9 rather have a Porsche. *(She pantomimes driving a Porsche, leaning*
10 *back, turning the wheel.)*
11   Clarisse, is this a hat shop or a museum? Where did you
12 get all these weird hats? Never mind, I love it. I can't believe
13 the things that are in. I guess it doesn't matter what you wear
14 as long as it is right for you — that is, if you can wear it with
15 style. But I just can't wear a bonnet. *(She returns bonnet to rack*
16 *and takes an elaborate turban, fitting it on carefully, turning before*
17 *the imaginary mirror.)*
18   Oh, la-di-da! Now if I were on my way to Iran! They'd
19 never be able to tell me apart from the Ayotollah. I could wear
20 my graduation robe with it and be in holy ceremonial dress.
21 *(She folds her hands in front of her and strolls slowly, bowing her*
22 *head to "acknowledge" worshippers.)*
23   Where do we wear something like this? To church or to a
24 plutonium auction? Hey, wouldn't heavy loop earrings be
25 perfect with this? I'm ready, Mr. President. Send me off to
26 Tehran, and I'll take care of delicate international matters in
27 proper attire. Or, this hat should be just the trick for the
28 president himself on his next peace-keeping tour. Maybe I
29 should buy one and send it to him. *(She returns turban to rack*
30 *and selects a traditional beret. It is a round, flat cap, preferably in felt.)*
31   Oh, a beret! I need this to wear with my bagpipes. *(She*
32 *pantomimes bagpipes by puffing out her cheeks and gesturing the*
33 *filling of bags.)* Of course, I would need a kilt. Or maybe golf
34 bags. *(Swings an imaginary club.)* Or maybe just to be la
35 Parisienne on the streets of Paris. *(Pronounced Pa-ree)*

1   Oh, I like this. Besides, when I get tired of it, I can use it
2 to carry a pie to the potluck. Neat, simple, versatile, never out
3 of style. Clarisse, do you have the beret in other colors? I could
4 use several of these. *(She lays the beret aside on chair or table and*
5 *takes a traditional sailor straw or bowler from the rack. It has a flat*
6 *top and brim.)*
7   Now this, they call a sailor or a boater or a bowler. One
8 descended from the other; I don't know in what order. I never
9 saw a sailor wear one of these. Little girls, maybe, or little boys,
10 but no sailors. I wonder what a sailor would think if you put
11 this on his head. *(She tries it on, adjusting several times.)*
12   And I don't look a bit like a sailor. I might join a barber
13 shop quartet, though. *(Sings.)* Sweet Adeline. My Adeline!
14 *(Speaks.)* Oh, I need a cane. *(She struts and kicks a quartet routine.)*
15   For you I pine, my Adeline. But not very much. I guess
16 this one is not for me. *(She returns hat to rack and selects a large-*
17 *brimmed straw picture hat exaggerated in size but attractive.)*
18   Here's one for me! Now, this is a hat. I could use it for an
19 umbrella. *(Pantomimes protecting herself from the rain.)* Or I could
20 be a table and use this in the center to keep the sun off the
21 lemonade. Or I could stretch out on the beach without suntan
22 lotion. How about a hat dance? *(She puts hat on the floor and does*
23 *a hat dance step around it and on its brim.)*
24   La cucaracha, la cucaracha! It's OK, Clarisse. I'm going
25 to take this one for sure. What do you call this — garden hat?
26 Sombrero? Parasol? Picture hat? Whatever, I want it. Put it on
27 my account. *(She tries it on before mirror and adjusts it becomingly.)*
28   Now where can I wear this? To the movies? No, they
29 couldn't see from the next row. To the beach? I'd lose it in the
30 wind. To dinner? The waiter wouldn't be able to reach my plate.
31 I know. To church. I'll wear it to church. There's always plenty
32 of room at church. *(She "models" it smartly, turning before mirror*
33 *in satisfaction.)*
34   Wherever I wear it, it will make a statement. Of course it's
35 not so much what's on your head as what's in it if you want to

1   make a statement. And you need someone to pay attention if
2   you have something important to say. Well, at least this will
3   get everyone's attention while I'm trying to think of something
4   to say.
5   Clarisse, you've made my day. Call me when you get some
6   new hats. *(She picks up her purse and walks out, a model of good*
7   *taste and confidence.)*
8
9
10
11
12
13
14
15
16
17
18
19
20
21
22
23
24
25
26
27
28
29
30
31
32
33
34
35

10. ALONA

PRODUCTION NOTES

SET: A kitchen in a middle-class home. The most effective arrangement allows for the actor to move about with back to audience Upstage as if at a sink and counter and to sit at a small table facing the audience at about Center Stage.

LIGHTS: Early evening interior.

SOUND: No background sound is necessary.

PROPS: Props can be pantomimed except for four cups and saucers. It is important that audience see the placement of cups and saucers twice — suggesting Alona's sense of the presence of a second party each time. All else may be pantomimed.

COSTUME: Alona wears neat and becoming casual clothing such as a woman would wear in her own home. Clothing should not be dated or stereotyped.

PLAYING TIME: Nine minutes.

CAST: Alona is a graying widow of fifty or more. She has a positive attitude about growing old but is lonely. She exhibits a range of emotions from casual good humor to remembered anguish and thoughtful profundity.

AT RISE: Alona stands at the kitchen sink, back to audience. She is washing dishes. Pantomime must be precise without detracting from what she is saying. She turns slowly and speaks as soon as lights focus.

1　　　Tom? You know what she said, Tom? *(She dries dishes and*
2　*puts them away, directing speech toward one of the chairs at the table.)*
3　She said, "Alona, you are talking to yourself." And I said, "No,
4　I'm not. Just because you can't see the person I'm talking to
5　doesn't mean there is no one there."
6　　　And then she said, "Alona, please talk to Dr. Frank about
7　it. You can talk to Dr. Frank." Well, she's right there. I can talk
8　to him, but he doesn't talk back. He just sits there and fiddles
9　with his pen and pays no attention to me. What's worse, talking
10　to a man who's completely visible but doesn't listen or to an
11　invisible one who does?
12　　　I'd rather talk to you, Tom. *(She sets two visible cups and*
13　*saucers on the table.)* You didn't always listen when you sat here
14　across the table from me — when I could see you — but now
15　you are very attentive. *(Laughs.)* Got you there, Dear! Now I
16　can guarantee that you will listen and even answer the way I'd
17　like you to. Never could do that while you were alive. *(She*
18　*pantomimes pouring coffee, returning pot to counter. Her cheerful mood*
19　*alters with each line in the next three speeches. She expresses loss,*
20　*frustration, anger, resignation.)*
21　　　I wish I had gone ahead and said what I was thinking
22　when you were tailing that truck. *(She sits.)* But I had said it
23　often enough, and you never paid any attention anyway. You
24　weren't mean about it — just were going to see how close you
25　could come no matter what. Well, you couldn't go that close.
26　He did hit his brakes. That's one time I should have been
27　bugging you.
28　　　And Tom, I'm going to say this now . . . a bit late. You were
29　an intelligent man — a reasonable man most of the time. Yet
30　you were willing to gamble lives — mine and yours and the
31　truck driver's — on a dare. On dare-devil behavior. Why? Why?
32　Life is so precious. You could still be alive. You have a
33　grandchild now. Think what you are missing. What we are
34　missing. We could have retired eventually and traveled.
35　Enjoyed having the house paid for. Gone deep-sea fishing.

1   Skiing. All the things we had worked for. It is still hard to
2   forgive you. *(Pause)*
3   I think you knew, in that split second, because you did a
4   remarkable thing. You turned the wheel to the right instead of
5   left. You gave me a chance. It meant I lived.
6   I lived, but part of me died with you. *(Long pause. She rises,*
7   *dries dishes. She has regained her composure when she speaks.)*
8   Oh, yes. I was talking about Nettie. She means well, but
9   she doesn't have any idea what it is like to be alone. Her kids
10   are gone, so she thinks she's alone. Ben there every night. Even
11   her mom living with them. She thinks I'm cracking up because
12   I talk to you. And to Tommy and Betty Lou. Oh, they call me
13   now and then and send Mother's Day cards. That's fine. They
14   are OK. They have their lives to live, and I still have mine. So
15   I talk to them every day without bothering them or running up
16   a phone bill. And I'm amazed at the maturity and wisdom of
17   their conversations! *(Laughs.)*
18   Yes, it's lonely. But being a widow is not all bad — once I
19   accepted the fact that you were gone. I've had to learn, of
20   course, not to feel sorry for myself. Learn how to make it all
21   work. And talking to people I can't see helps to make it work.
22   Better sometimes than having live bodies around. Less cooking!
23   Don't be offended, Dear. I'd rather have you here than anyone
24   in the world, but you aren't in the world, so what's second best?
25   I can pretend. Seems normal to me. *(She is cheerful again. She is*
26   *deliberately entertaining herself and Tom.)*
27   Oh, I want to tell you about this. There was a man here
28   the other day — a repairman to fix the garage door opener. It
29   is one of the few things I haven't been able to fix for myself.
30   Tom, you won't believe this. This man says, "Ma'am, do you
31   have a screwdriver I could use?" This so-called expert — you
32   know, one with a leather apron full of tools come to fix a gadget
33   which requires tools, and he doesn't have a screwdriver! Well,
34   I got one out of the drawer and handed it to him.
35   "Oh, no, Ma'am," he says. "I need a Phillips." Well, there

1   is one in your tool box in the garage, so I start out to get it. But
2   he stops me to give this little lecture so I'll know what to look
3   for — this expert. "A Phillips, Ma'am, is a screwdriver with a
4   double bite on it."
5   I stop, then, to listen to this wise, incredibly well-informed
6   man, and he thinks I don't understand. "You see," he says, "it
7   is a special tool which handles a screw like this one." He shows
8   me a Phillips screw, then, as if demonstrating a miraculous
9   new discovery of science. "You see, it is cut twice instead of
10   once on the head. This is the head, this flat part. It requires a
11   special tool for handling."
12   So, Tom, I listen with a straight face. I listen and nod and
13   say, "Now isn't that interesting." I guess I should have said,
14   "Of course I know what a Phillips screwdriver is, Mr. Idiot,"
15   but I didn't. You would have loved that scene. I got the Phillips
16   for him and had a good laugh while he worked in the garage.
17   You know what I do? Every now and then I repeat that scene
18   to myself for entertainment. It's good for a lot of laughs. *(She*
19   *laughs.)* I really enjoy that little drama. Ah, there is such wisdom
20   among the experts.
21   How does a guy like that think I got this far in life? How
22   does he think I turned gray without learning a few things? Why
23   do you think that the older I get the less I'm expected to know?
24   Is it because there is no man around who would be privy to
25   such treasured bits of knowledge? Or do these experts think
26   that the fading of my hair color means the fading of my brain?
27   Or is it that all widows are supposed to be helpless?
28   Remember when your brother thought he needed to teach
29   me how to replace a washer in a leaking faucet? . . . Tom, you
30   are not listening. Tom? Well, that's OK. I'll talk to you later. I'll
31   visit with Dad for awhile. *(She faces opposite direction and*
32   *"discovers" another guest.)*
33   Well, look who's here! Hi, Dad! You haven't stopped by in
34   a long time. Sit down, sit down. Coffee? *(She removes two cups*
35   *from table and replaces them with two more, then reaches for imaginary*

1   *pot and pours.)* **Just a pinch of sugar?** *(She serves it.)* **Just the**
2   **way you like it.**
3   **You look great, Dad! How's Mother?** *(She sits in the chair*
4   *"vacated" by Tom.)* **Well, it's good to have a chance to talk to you.**
5   **I'll see her later.**
6   **You look better than you did at seventy. Your handsome**
7   **white hair. Do you suppose I'm going to take after you? I'd love**
8   **it if my hair looks like that. I miss you, Dad. Everyone always**
9   **says, "I know you miss Tom," and I do. But Dad, I miss you,**
10   **too. And Mom. I'm glad you don't mind these one-voice**
11   **conversations. I know you understand. Did you talk to Mother**
12   **a lot after she was gone? I'll bet you did. It makes sense, doesn't**
13   **it? All the things we didn't get to say then we have time to say**
14   **now.**
15   **Every day I think of something you said when I was**
16   **growing up — some of those times when you thought I wasn't**
17   **listening. I heard everything you said about being true to**
18   **myself. Doing what my talents suggested. Doing things for**
19   **myself. It pays off now — independence. You taught me to be**
20   **independent. Oh, I don't change a flat tire out on the highway.**
21   **Remember you made me learn to do that before you would let**
22   **me drive? Well nowadays it's rare for a tire to go flat, and it's**
23   **not safe anymore to get out on a freeway and change one, but**
24   **I remember how. I could do it if I had to.**
25   **Being independent, you said, meant being alone**
26   **sometimes. I think it was Emerson you quoted — you were**
27   **always quoting Emerson — "We walk alone in the world." But**
28   **most of that wisdom was yours. You also said that no matter**
29   **how many people are around, each of us is always alone. Learn**
30   **to be alone, you said, learn to take care of yourself.**
31   **But the most important part I'm still trying to learn to do.**
32   **You said, "Keep company with your soul and you'll never be**
33   **lonely." I guess what you meant was that if you can accept**
34   **yourself and believe in your own significance — your unique**
35   **and solitary personal value — if you can talk to yourself when**

1   you're alone — and listen — you'll be OK.

2   Only for me, I have to pretend it's you or Tom or one of

3   the kids I'm talking to. Talking to my soul seems a bit awesome.

4   I don't think I'm quite ready for that. Oh, I know you could do

5   it. But I'm still talking to Tom. And you. My soul and I are still

6   getting acquainted. It's making itself known a little at a time.

7   I think when I get over Tom's terrible sacrifice of his own life

8   I can think about my soul. I'll probably do that by the time I'm

9   seventy. Eighty, maybe.

10   And when we are on good terms — my soul and I — I'll be

11   ready for the big loneliness. It won't be so bad — might even

12   be wonderful if I experience it a little at a time. Keep in practice.

13   Talk to you and Mother and Tom. Souls. *(She sits quietly, closes*

14   *her eyes, hugs herself. She is trying to communicate with her soul.*

15   *Then she looks up as if remembering she has a guest.)*

16   **More coffee?** *(She pantomimes pouring two cups while lights*

17   *dim to out.)* **Just a pinch of sugar?**

18

19

20

21

22

23

24

25

26

27

28

29

30

31

32

33

34

35

11. PROFESSOR CYBELE

PRODUCTION NOTES

SET: A professional office. A desk at approximately right angles to the audience at Center Stage and a swivel desk chair are needed; other items may be added at the discretion of the director.

LIGHTS: Interior daylight.

SOUND: Telephone bell.

PROPS: Briefcase, telephone, folders and papers, box of tissues.

COSTUME: Professor Cybele is impeccably dressed in a business suit and smart shoes. Her hair is cut short or tightly coiffured. She wears a watch.

PLAYING TIME: Six minutes.

CAST: Professor Cybele* is thirty-five to forty years old, astute, confident, and capable of handling any situation in her command. She wastes not a minute in organizing her desk and her thoughts. A surprising circumstance revealed through a telephone conversation introduces contrasts in her personality.

AT RISE: Professor Cybele enters and walks briskly to her desk. The telephone is ringing. She looks at her watch and picks up the phone, opening her briefcase and removing papers as she answers the call.

* *Cybele: "Great Mother" in ancient Syrian mythology.*

1   Good morning. Cybele *(Sĭ-bél)* here. Yes, this is Dr. Cybele.
2   No, my secretary doesn't arrive for another hour.
3   No problem, Mr. Staunch.
4   Yes, I have your invitation. *(She looks through papers.)* **Just**
5   haven't had time to respond. Need to give it a little thought.
6   *(She picks up a letter and studies it.)*
7   Society for Social Concerns on the ninth? Not much
8   preparation time. But the range of topics you have suggested
9   gives me a wide choice. Let's see: overpopulation, depletion of
10   natural resources, economic burden of third-world advances,
11   birth control — right or responsibility.
12   Sounds as if I should just combine all the world's problems
13   into one and solve it in forty-five minutes while Social Concerns
14   members enjoy their chablis and oysters on the half shell.
15   *(Laughter)* Do you have a preference? What focus would you
16   like?
17   Very good. I'll give it some thought. When do you need
18   my decision, yesterday?
19   Yes, that's fine. I'll let you know. Thanks for your
20   invitation. *(She replaces telephone, lays out papers on desk, sits, turns*
21   *swivel chair to face audience, studies the letter again. She speaks as*
22   *she moves.)*
23   Old flattery approach when they're short on time and
24   money. Wonder what man turned them down. *(She reads.)*
25   "...want to hear from a woman who has been everywhere,
26   one who knows academia and the corporate world, one who
27   understands social issues. We know of no one else with your
28   impressive credentials and would be proud to have you address
29   the Society for Social Concerns at our next meeting."
30   Blah, blah, blah. Why don't they just say, "We couldn't get
31   the man who was our first choice, so you'll do if we can get you
32   at this late date."
33   But maybe by default I can do some good. Population
34   explosion. Population control. That's the gist of it. They want
35   me to choose a topic as long as it is birth control. They are

1   right, of course. **The problems of humankind in one word:**
2   **overpopulation.** *(She laughs, turns back to her desk, sorts papers.)*
3   **Not funny, Cindy Cybele.** *(She clearly is amused.)* **I guess I**
4   **could do it since it is so soon.** *(Telephone rings. She answers.)*
5   **Cybele here.... No.... Yes.... Never felt better....**
6   **Lunch? Sorry, Mandy, I'm booked. Not tomorrow either. AAUW**
7   **at noon. Academic Senate Thursday. Corporate council Friday.**
8   **Let's try next week. Thanks, Mandy. Bye.** *(She replaces phone,*
9   *picks up clipboard, pen and paper. She stands, walks about, jots down*
10   *notes as she talks.)*
11   **Woman's right or responsibility? It would help if we could**
12   **make women see their duty to solve it all — under direction of**
13   **men, of course.** *(Sarcasm)* **Maybe I'm not being fair. I guess I**
14   **can't say it exactly that way.** *(She crosses out a note.)*
15   **I could do this one in my sleep. Environmental resources**
16   **under strain. Millions more to feed every day. Humanity on the**
17   **way to self-destruction. Not a matter of individual choice but**
18   **of individual responsibility.**
19   **That sounds good.** *(She writes.)* **It is good. If we could just**
20   **convince every man and woman on the planet not to have**
21   **children they don't want.** *(She laughs.)* **No, not every man —**
22   **every woman.** *(She takes off her suit coat and hangs it on her chair,*
23   *takes several tissues from the box on her desk, and pats her face and*
24   *neck. She continues to jot notes as she speaks.)*
25   **Women who want babies should have them. Those who**
26   **don't shouldn't. Nothing worse than a mother who doesn't want**
27   **to be a mother unless it is a woman who wants to be a mother**
28   **and can't.**
29   **Creation's finest miracle. Perpetuating life. Every woman**
30   **who wants to should be a part of the miracle.**
31   **I don't think this is what they expect to hear, but I'm going**
32   **to say it. One child per willing woman — no more. In two**
33   **generations the population would begin to level off. How to get**
34   **that message heard and accepted is the issue.**
35   **First, women treated as equals would be women behaving**

1   as equals. More authority, more cooperation. If women are to
2   solve it, then women must be allowed to solve it. Not politicians.
3   Not the government. Not the church. Women with authority,
4   men cooperating. *(Telephone rings.)*
5   Good morning. Cybele here. *(She smiles, sits, leans back in*
6   *her chair.)* Good morning, Darling. *(Her manner changes completely*
7   *from that of the efficient executive and academic to that of the woman*
8   *in love.)*
9   You know the answer to that. I feel like a teenager. No.
10 Better. A teenager would probably be scared. I'm awed but not
11 afraid. *(Her voice is soft and melodious.)* Blessed. Privileged.
12 Grateful. Supremely happy.
13   I'm glad you do, because regardless of how you feel, I'm
14 elated. I'm a robin on wing in spring!
15   I haven't thought about that yet. Let the corporate world
16 and academia take care of themselves. I guess they did before
17 Cindy Cybele came on the scene. They'll get along without me
18 until I'm ready to come back.
19   Listen to this. *(She picks up letter.)* The Society for Social
20 Concerns wants me to lecture next Wednesday on population
21 control. Isn't that rich?! *(She laughs.)* Yes, I think I'll do it. Their
22 goals are lofty and absolutely on target even if their timing is
23 bad. I'm sure someone turned them down, but if they were
24 allowing me another six weeks I'd have to say no.
25   You know how I feel about that. Of all the miracles of
26 nature, it is the most wonderful, and we are a part of it. It
27 couldn't have happened to Professor Cybele. Remember what
28 that medic said, "Sorry, but the two of you — no."
29   Yes, Sweetheart. I'll give the lecture. I'll let them know
30 today. Then when I've said my piece, you and I will go shopping.
31 For a crib. And a teddy bear. *(She laughs with joy.)*
32   Gotta go. Eight o'clock lecture in five minutes. Love you.
33 bye. *(She replaces the phone, scatters papers on her desk, kicks off*
34 *her shoes. She does a kick step or two, flips her hair with her hands.*
35 *She gestures to demonstrate her anticipated shape and laughs again.*

1   *She is jubilant.)*
2   **A baby! A real live little person. Professor Cybele is going**
3   **to have a baby!** *(Lights go out.)*
4
5
6
7
8
9
10
11
12
13
14
15
16
17
18
19
20
21
22
23
24
25
26
27
28
29
30
31
32
33
34
35

12. DUENNA

PRODUCTION NOTES

SET: The stage is empty except for a railroad crossing gate Downstage parallel to the apron, suggesting that a railroad track separates the audience from the actor. The gate arm can be stationary, but its effectiveness is much enhanced if it can be dropped and raised as script indicates. Other set items such as a railroad crossing sign on a pedestal at Downstage Right facing away from the audience may be used but are not essential.

LIGHTS: Lighting is simple but important. Bright outdoor daylight is used except for a few seconds during the suggestion of a passing freight train at which time lights go out completely.

SOUND: Taped sound effects of a train whistle in the distance, approaching train, and passing train are essential.

PROPS: Large shopping bag or tote bag.

COSTUME: Duenna wears attractive spring clothing: a full-skirted, light-weight dress, dainty shoes, and a big summer hat. The dress skirt should have pockets. She wears a watch.

PLAYING TIME: Four minutes or less.

CAST: Duenna* is a graceful, attractive, eccentric woman in her forties or fifties (or younger). She moves like a dancer. She converses with invisible angels as if it were entirely logical to do so.

AT RISE: Duenna strolls On-stage as if enjoying a spring morning. She is humming or singing to herself. After a little whirl and a small leap, she stops about Stage Center and speaks to her invisible friends.

* *duenna: governess, chaperone.*

1   **Isn't it a beautiful morning?! Fresh and sweet. A perfect**
2   **day for a walk in the park. Wait a minute.** *(She gestures as if to*
3   *hold back eager walkers.)* **We'll cross as soon as it's safe.**

4   **Come, little ones. Come close to me, cherubs. This can be**
5   **dangerous. Come. Come.** *(She gestures as if gathering children close*
6   *to her, using her skirt and her hat, moving about in a large circle as*
7   *if in a dance.)*

8   **Here, hop into my pocket. Or here, the shopping bag is**
9   **roomy. Oh, yes, there's room for you, too.** *(She lifts weightless*
10   *angels and slips them into bag and pockets.)*

11   **Want to ride in my hat? Come on little fellow, fold your**
12   **wings and hop in!** *(She dips her hat to the stage floor and circles it,*
13   *stepping lightly, then lifts it carefully and places it on her head.)*

14   **There's room for everyone who wants a lift!**

15   **Here, precious, you may sit on my shoulder.** *(She laughs.)*
16   **An angel on her shoulder! Hey, don't tickle my ears like that**
17   **or you'll walk the rest of the way!** *(Sound of distant warning*
18   *whistle of approaching train is heard.)*

19   **Oh! That's the 8:07 about two minutes early!** *(She looks at*
20   *her watch. If functional gate is used, it drops into place at this point,*
21   *separating actor from audience.)*

22   **Come close, everyone! Hurry! Hurry! Here. Here.** *(She*
23   *circles the stage gathering imaginary angels hurriedly into her skirt,*
24   *pockets, the shopping bag, and her range of protection.)*

25   **We'll have to hurry before someone tries to lead me away**
26   **again. They just don't understand that you and I look after**
27   **each other. Here you are protecting us all the time, and we**
28   **visible creatures never try to take care of you angels.**

29   **Come on! Come on.** *(Her gathering and protecting gestures*
30   *continue as she speaks in conversational manner as if angels are*
31   *responding.)*

32   **We worldly folks have a tendency to ignore other-worldly**
33   **beings. We don't have any trouble believing in invisible**
34   **concepts like tomorrow or love or our rights, but for some**
35   **reason we hesitate to acknowledge factors outside our range**

1 of experience — like presence of angels or of those who live on
2 the other side of the world. If we can't understand it or are
3 uncomfortable with it, we sometimes just look the other way.
4 *(Noise of train increases. She suddenly leaps toward the tracks as if*
5 *someone were there.)*
6   No! No! Come back! Come back, little one! The train is
7 coming! Jump! Jump! Fly! *(Train noise is at its peak. She runs*
8 *under the gate and down the tracks toward approaching train Stage*
9 *Left, stepping as if from one tie to another, reaching out for a small*
10 *angel.)*
11   Come back! Wait! *(Lights go out suddenly. Noise of train*
12 *passing continues for a few seconds. During black-out, actor returns*
13 *to Center Stage and stands so that gate again separates her from*
14 *audience. Lights go on suddenly as train sound decreases. She stands*
15 *calmly watching the train disappear off Right. She holds an "angel"*
16 *against her shoulder as if holding a baby, rocking back and forth*
17 *gently, patting and reassuring it. Train noise fades out.)*
18   There. It's gone. It's gone, and you are fine. We are all OK.
19 We looked after each other. It's OK. It's OK. *(The gate is lifted*
20 *quickly if it is rigged to move. If not, she goes around it and crosses*
21 *the "tracks" into the audience, gesturing to make sure that all her*
22 *angel friends come with her. She speaks as she exits.)*
23   Come on. We are all safe now. Come, little ones, let's get
24 to the park and watch the birds have breakfast. Take your
25 buddy's hand. Let's take care of each other. Come on, now. Off
26 to springtime we go. *(Lights go out.)*
27
28
29
30
31
32
33
34
35

13. SERINA

PRODUCTION NOTES

SET: An empty stage will do. The action takes place at a large family gathering in a hotel dining room or a church recreational room. A wheelchair is needed. The audience is the family.

LIGHTS: Soft daylight, interior.

SOUND: Group singing of "Happy Birthday" and group applause.

PROPS: No props are necessary.

COSTUME: Serina is dressed in neat, becoming clothing appropriate for an elderly woman of reasonable means. Her hair is fashionably dressed. She should not be stereotyped in any way.

PLAYING TIME: Ten minutes.

CAST: Serina is ninety years old, a beautiful, wrinkled, white-haired lady, serene, confident, and articulate. She is not a caricature of senility, but is a wise and loving person with a sense of humor who has experienced hardship and ease, simplicity and grandeur. Her very presence inspires interest and respect. She speaks almost intimately to the audience as if to family members at her birthday party.

AT RISE: The sound of "Happy Birthday" may begin while the stage is still dark. Applause should die down as Serina maneuvers herself onto stage in a wheelchair or simply faces the audience as lights go up.

1   Well, now that we've all had our cake — my cake, wasn't
2 it? I guess since it's my birthday it's my cake. But the only way
3 to enjoy cake is to share it, so be sure you've all had a piece.
4   Thanks for helping me blow out the candles, children. My
5 wishes always come true anyway. I'm not even wishing for
6 another birthday; it'll be nice if I get one, but I guess I've had
7 my share. I'll do my best to be here next year, but if I can't, I'm
8 grateful for the first ninety.
9   And now according to the Reverend Michael James, my
10 first grandson, *(She acknowledges him in the audience)* I'm to say
11 something everyone will remember for years and years to come.
12 Something wise. Something profound. You see, I'm expected
13 to be wise because of my ninety years of living. Well, just
14 existing doesn't make a person wise, but learning from
15 everything around us, laughing a bit, working hard at what we
16 do best, playing now and then, and loving a lot — those are the
17 things that make one wise. Does that sound profound, Michael
18 James?
19   Oh, yes, and listening, of course. Listening is like praying.
20 We have to listen to understand what we hope for. When I
21 taught in a one-room school — oh, yes, I did, Jeremy — one
22 room, grades one through eight. When I taught in a one-room
23 school the tyke who sat in the corner and listened without
24 showing off was the one who became governor.
25   We all know you are here, Jeremy; you may sit down now.
26 It's my turn to show off a bit. Good. That's better.
27   If you really try to listen, to work hard, and to love,
28 especially to love, you find out that the truth — the real truth
29 about things — is not so hard to come by. No one knows all the
30 answers, not the scientists, not the holy men, not the teachers.
31 Sometimes the children do, or maybe the poets, but usually not
32 people somewhere between junior high school and the first
33 credit card — not the ones who think they know it all. And the
34 grandparents don't know it all either.
35   Well, we know more than some folks give us credit for.

1   We've been here taking it all in for longer than some of you
2   can even imagine. Oh, yes, sometimes my forgetter works better
3   than my rememberer, but that happens to everybody — not just
4   great-grandmas. I'm no different from the rest of you except
5   that I've been here longer.

6   Contrary to what you may be thinking right now, Dannielle,
7   unless it is diseased, the brain does not deteriorate with age;
8   instincts do not diminish. The need for love and companionship
9   does not decrease just because you've lived a long time. I still
10 understand when a woman walks across the room in high heels
11 and a tight leather skirt. The normal process is for wisdom to
12 increase with experience, sex to improve with practice, memory
13 to intensify with use.

14   Don't be uncomfortable, Danni. At twenty-one you may
15 find that hard to believe, but that's because you've had only
16 twenty-one years in which to learn. And your leather skirt is
17 smashing, Honey.

18   All that deterioration can take place, of course, if you
19 accept yourself as some kind of caricature or stereotype of age.
20 You don't have to be what others are programmed to believe
21 you are.

22   Now, just being old doesn't make you wonderful, either.
23 It's not so remarkable to live a long time and to have several
24 generations of descendants. How many greats am I now? Three
25 or four? It isn't that I forget, it's just that it doesn't matter —
26 several generations of children and their children and theirs
27 related to me — that's not so remarkable. Most human beings
28 are capable of creating offspring. The thing that's remarkable
29 in my case is that all my children and grandchildren are
30 beautiful and brilliant. All perfect. *(She waits a moment, watching*
31 *for a response, then laughs.)*
32   Well, if you aren't going to laugh at my jokes, I'll have to.
33 Perfect people. If we were all perfect we'd be a tiresome crowd.
34 We can change the hair style or the church membership, but
35 we aren't going to reach perfection. Maybe it is just as well.

1   We need to learn to accept ourselves as we are and to like
2   ourselves. There is nothing like believing in oneself to help
3   acquire confidence and to do a better job of whatever we do.
4   Margie, now, and cinnamon apple pie. Margie believes she's
5   number one at apple pies, and she is. She's also close to the
6   top with computer maneuvers, and she knows it. I don't know
7   why you like those talking typewriters with green faces, Margie,
8   but I salute your self-confidence.
9   Let's see. We were talking about perfection. Well, who's
10   to decide what human perfection might be? Candice — what
11   are you now, eighteen? Candice here in her teenage beauty but
12   with not too much experience yet at, say, balancing her
13   checkbook, or Grace Ellen who at forty-eight has earned her
14   first few wrinkles? Who's to say wrinkles don't make us more
15   beautiful?
16   You are lovely, Candice, but your mom is lovelier because
17   of all the wrinkles she's earned staying awake nights praying
18   you were OK when you didn't come home on time. And your
19   grandmother Gloria is even prettier with that silver crown of
20   serenity she wears. She's had two generations of staying awake
21   at night and hoping two generations of you are OK.
22   Serenity. Serenity at seventy is a kind of beauty we all
23   should strive for. People who aren't afraid to grow old and are
24   happy with their lives at any age are beautiful people. You earn
25   your wrinkles, you know. If you are wise you will wear them
26   without apology. *(She rolls her chair slightly to Left of Center,*
27   *focusing on two teenage great grandsons.)*
28   Eddie, quit upstaging me! You've learned a lot in your
29   sixteen years, haven't you? So much that you really don't need
30   to listen to this old lady. And John? You are finding out what
31   life is all about. Cars. Girls. Money. Weird hair cuts. And you
32   know all kinds of things your dad and mom can't possibly know.
33   How could they? They are old — at least forty! Well, let me tell
34   you something, dudes. Multiply sixteen by two and a half and
35   then double the number. That's ninety-six, and that's eighty

1 years more experience and know-how than you have had, and
2 don't you forget it. Your parents have been sixteen and nineteen
3 and twenty-nine and thirty-nine. And by the way, Great Granny
4 was sixteen once herself. You haven't seen anything she doesn't
5 know about. *(She turns away from John and Eddie.)*
6   Never could understand why the younger you are the less
7 everyone else knows. And none of it worth paying attention to.
8   Well, if you had been listening, you two, I wouldn't have
9 had to include the lecture. All right. Back to wise thoughts for
10 everybody. *(She rolls back toward Center, speaking as she moves.)*
11   Don't try to solve all the world's problems. Tackle one or
12 two where you know you can make a difference and work hard
13 on them. Head up the campaign to recycle aluminum cans and
14 don't let a single one clutter the roadside. Complain loudly
15 about an oil spill. Go out and help clean it up yourself. Speak
16 up about population control. When you've done what you can,
17 relax and play for awhile. Go skiing. Play checkers. But play.
18 You listen especially to this one, Reverend Michael James.
19 There is just so much we can do, and one way to get the strength
20 to do it is to play now and then. If the Creator hadn't meant
21 for us to play, there wouldn't be squirrels with big saucy tails
22 to tease the cats with. *(She acknowledges a child facing her at close
23 range.)*
24   That is kinda funny, isn't it, Lucy? Of course you may
25 laugh at Grandma. If we could all giggle like that we'd never
26 have bad colds! *(She pauses a minute, rethinking what she has said.)*
27   Love life. Did I say that? Love life. I don't think that's in
28 the Bible just that way, Michael James. And it sounds too simple
29 to be profound. It doesn't matter. It's in lots of other good books.
30 Love life. That means, of course, value it. Protect it. Enjoy it.
31 Be grateful for every little firefly and each huge trumpeting
32 elephant. Welcome new experiences. Read. A good book is still
33 better than TV. Your brain is better at creating the picture than
34 any camera is.
35   And fall in love. When you love, say so. Oh, go ahead and

1 say so. Saying you love helps you understand what you mean.
2 Understanding how to love is becoming lovable.
3   And the more love you share, the more grateful you should
4 be that for some reason, you've lived long enough to really love.
5 When your time is up, be ready, because death is a part of
6 living, too. You all pay attention when I die. I won't be making
7 a speech, and I'll do the best I can to make it a good death.
8   Cry a little, because we will miss each other, but laugh,
9 too, because without laughter we couldn't tolerate dying, could
10 we?
11   I've said enough, Michael James. It is still nice outside. I
12 think I'll watch the fireflies for awhile. They flash little messages
13 to us all the time.
14   Come with me, Lucy, Terry. You can take turns riding
15 with Granny in this big chair. *(Lights go out slowly as she backs*
16 *her chair away from the audience.)*
17
18
19
20
21
22
23
24
25
26
27
28
29
30
31
32
33
34
35

Men
Characters

Photo by Sarah Foltz

Jonny Hofmann as "BACCHUS"

14. BACCHUS

PRODUCTION NOTES

SET: A hospital waiting room. Two or three pieces of typical waiting room furniture will suggest the setting and provide for variety in movement of the actor. "Quiet" and "No Smoking" signs may be used on the backdrop.

LIGHTS: Soft, interior, after midnight. Spot at conclusion.

SOUND: No background sound is necessary. A cymbal crash can be used at conclusion.

PROPS: Two beer cans, magazines — one with the photo of a model on the cover, cigarette lighter, matches, cigarettes, pocket comb.

COSTUME: Bacchus is dressed in clothing of a contemporary teenager, perhaps a T-shirt, jeans (splashed with blood), a denim or leather jacket with inside pockets, baseball cap, and running shoes or high-tops with laces dangling.

PLAYING TIME: Ten minutes.

CAST: Bacchus* is almost eighteen. He is good looking, cocky, and sure of himself, at first quite appealing. He frequently flashes a big smile, helping to project the enigmatic effect of both innocence and guilt. He walks about in a fashion somewhere between strutting and pacing, sitting occasionally, moving from one seat to another, talking to himself (not to audience).

AT RISE: Bacchus is strolling around the waiting room. He is restless but strides assuredly as if he has all under control. He glances at magazines, tosses them aside.

* *Bacchus: Greek and Roman mythological god of wine and fertility.*

1   You'd think they'd have an ashtray in this place. Nothing
2   to do but look at **Ladies' Home Journal.** *(He takes out a pack of*
3   *cigarettes, taps them, returns them to his jacket.)*
4   Two or three hours, they said. Two or three doctors and
5   a dozen flunkies in those gray pajamas and it takes two or three
6   hours?
7   And the cop said I could stay here but can't go nowhere
8   else. OK. OK. I'll stay, but I don't see why they need me. I'm
9   not hurt. *(He walks full width of stage and looks Off-stage as if*
10 *making sure no one is watching him. Then he takes a can of beer from*
11 *inside his jacket and opens it. He takes a long drink.)*
12 Trooper said, "No booze in there. No booze." Didn't even
13 frisk my jacket. Real smart. So, what's a dude to do for three
14 hours? Talk to myself, I guess. *(He returns can to inside jacket*
15 *pocket.)*
16 I need a drink. I was in that smash-up, too. Nobody seems
17 to notice that I was in that. I'm OK, though. Takes more than
18 a little accident to shake up old Bacchus. *(He struts a few steps,*
19 *takes off his cap and combs his hair with care.)*
20 And she'll be OK. They'll be OK. *(Brushes at blood on jeans.)*
21 Little bit a blood. Those roll bars took care of us. Flipped twice,
22 and I'm standin' here talkin'.
23 She's tough, Denni. She'll be fine. And since the kid is
24 mine, he'll be OK, too. It's a boy. Has to be a boy. *(He walks*
25 *again, smiles, thinking about being a father. He snaps a match or*
26 *two.)* He'll look like his old man. *(Combs his hair again.)*
27 A little blood; that's all. He'll be OK. Another Bacchus.
28 Just horsin' around. *(As if explaining, justifying)* The cop
29 says this time I can't get off with an **M.I.P.** *(Minor in possession).*
30 I'm no minor anymore. He's wrong. I ain't eighteen yet. Course
31 he also said if the baby dies I'm in real trouble. Well, I didn't
32 buy no booze. It was Dad's. It was in the garage — cases of it.
33 I'm not eighteen yet. Can't pin that on me. Besides, it was just
34 beer. *(He alternately sits, stands, walks.)*
35 Nah. They never did nothin' when we totaled that van of

1   Gem's. I miss Gem, but I mean, he wasn't blessed like me. Mom
2   says, "blessed." Bacchus, god of booze and babies. That's me.
3   I can hold the booze. Nobody can hold more. I mean nobody.
4   Well, maybe Dad.
5   And I never been hurt. Oh, semi-mushed a couple of times
6   when someone else was drivin' — never when I had the wheel.
7   Gem was drivin' when he was done in.
8   That was a sorry scene. We give him a bad time about
9   drivin' like a drunk when he'd had only half a dozen beers. He
10   was a real weenie, Gem. He just couldn't cut it.
11   And they marched us through Juvi *(Juvenile court)* and
12   sent us home. His parents were a bit hostile for a year or so,
13   but it wasn't my fault. They shoulda taught him how to hold
14   his beer. He was blitzed on half a dozen beers, for Chris'sake.
15   And he was drivin'. Learner's permit. Nice guy, though. *(He*
16   *pauses, thinking.)*
17   But if the baby dies, I'm in trouble. *(Another pause)* Nah. I
18   didn't kill nobody. They won't hang a reckless homicide on me
19   for just screwin' around. I know it's a boy. I'll teach him from
20   day one to hold his beer.
21   Denni. She'll be OK. They didn't say nothin' about her
22   dyin'. She'll be OK. She's tough. Yeah. No homicide charges.
23   No room in the courts for kids who just mess up with a few
24   beers. It'll take 'em two years even to hear the case — if there
25   is a case. Didn't arrest me. No "right to remain silent" routine.
26   And she's not goin' to die.
27   She didn't want no beer tonight. "Not good for the baby,"
28   she kept sayin'. Finally got her to loosen up. One can of beer
29   not goin' to hurt nothin'. She needed a little confidence. *(He has*
30   *plenty. He struts, smooths his hair.)* She needed a drink. She'll be
31   OK. Typical female. *(He furtively takes another drink and returns*
32   *can to inside pocket.)*
33   Real frigid. Always sayin' she don't want a drink, I mean,
34   even when she needs it. She just don't understand she needs
35   it. Afraid she'll mess up some way. She always took it though.

1   Takes it. Bacchus don't give up easy.

2   Wonder if the cops told her old lady yet. She'll give me a
3   huge hassle. Always does. *(He mimics Denni's mother.)* "No,
4   Denise is not here. No, Denise can't talk to you." And then Denni
5   picks up the phone. She is there. Denni does want to talk to
6   me. Always wants to talk to me. *(Struts, grins.)*

7   My girl. She's a great mash. Little mamma. The old lady
8   says she won't let me near the baby. Hah, won't she be
9   surprised. *(He mimics again.)* "Quit school. Got no job. Got no
10 goals. Can't go near that baby." Well, we'll see about that. A
11 father's got rights. Old Judge Bently will see to that. He always
12 understands. Never let me down yet. I ain't no criminal. Old
13 lady wants to take care of the kid, OK, but I'll see my kid
14 whenever I want to.

15 Dudes that don't want to have anything to do with their
16 kids are jerks. They don't need to do nothin' but put up with
17 a few noisy females. Welfare will pay. I ain't married to nobody.
18 All you have to do is stay out of the way until you want to see
19 your kid.

20 Don't need to marry nobody. Then you got real responsi-
21 bility. She's a kid. Fifteen. Her parents are responsible for her.
22 Let them take care of their kid. They'll take care of Denni.

23 And I'll see my kid whenever I want to. He'll live. Yeah,
24 he'll live.

25 Denni, too. She didn't look too good when they took her
26 in, but she'll be OK. Hope her face ain't too messed up. *(Pause)*
27 Have to think about this if her face is messed up. *(Long pause)*
28 I don't want no girl with a messed-up face. *(He snaps a match,*
29 *finishes the can of beer, and puts the empty back into his jacket. He*
30 *thumbs through a magazine with photo of a model clearly visible on*
31 *the cover.)*

32 Lotsa good lookin' women around. *(Takes out cigarette*
33 *lighter and snaps it off and on.)*

34 Three hours. How is a guy supposed to last in this place
35 for three hours? No booze. No cigarettes. I only been here an

1 hour and already I'm goin' bonkers. *(He takes another can of beer*
2 *from opposite side of his jacket.)*
3   This is my last can. Two more hours on one beer? And if
4 I leave this place the jerk cops will take me in. Bet they're sittin'
5 outside waitin' for me to try.
6   All this waitin'. Like bein' in the slammer. Way to go. Way
7 to treat a guy who's flipped his Jeep twice. Neat wheels totaled.
8 His girl on the operating table. Baby on the way, maybe. Well,
9 for sure. *(Wipes his forehead, puts on his cap.)*
10   They said they'd save the kid if they could. Denni first,
11 they said. Then deliver the baby and do some work on her face.
12 Temporary. Do some more later.
13   Yeah, she'll be OK. Her mom's insurance will pay. No way
14 they can use mine, 'cause I got none. See, if you don't have it,
15 they can't make you pay. I'm fine. Not even scratched. I'm takin'
16 care of myself. Bacchus is a lucky dude. "Propitious," Mom
17 says. I know some big words. Don't need no diploma.
18   Oh yeah, I got insurance on the Jeep. They're goin' to ask
19 me that. Neat wheels like that — of course I got insurance on
20 my car. Besides, the law says you gotta insure your vehicle. I
21 obey the law. Don't make you insure no passenger in this state.
22 Passenger's responsibility. Sounds fair.
23   What'll I name the kid? The guys said Hooch Junior. Very
24 funny. Bacchus the Second? Can't wait to see if he looks like
25 his old man. *(He removes the cap and combs his hair again.)*
26   He'll be OK. My kid'll be OK. *(He flashes a big grin which*
27 *fades quickly.)* And if he ain't, I'll have another. Nothing to it.
28 I'm good!
29   Man, when I get outta here, we'll celebrate. Get a keg or
30 two. Maybe find a couple of cases in Dad's garage. That judge
31 ain't goin' to do nothin'. I won't be eighteen for another month.
32 Nothin' they can do but send me back to Juvi even if she dies.
33 If he dies. Nobody's fault. I had roll bars and all.
34   Got no wheels for awhile, but I'll get wheels. Dad'll be
35 glad I'm not hurt. He'll get me new wheels.

1   **A new Wrangler** *(or other)*, **maybe.** *(Spotlight begins slow*
2 *focus on him as he visualizes and describes his new car with gestures*
3 *and body language.)* **Oversized wheels. Fog lights. Radical**
4 **custom paint job with, like, explosions all over it. Yeah! Killer**
5 **supertruck with Bacchus on the stick! Awesome!** *(He raises the*
6 *can of beer in salute as lights go out. Cymbal crash may also be used.)*
7
8
9
10
11
12
13
14
15
16
17
18
19
20
21
22
23
24
25
26
27
28
29
30
31
32
33
34
35

15. GUSTO BUOYANT

PRODUCTION NOTES

SET: The act takes place in the courtyard of a mall. No scenery is necessary, but a bench or a potted plant may be used to suggest the location unless the acrobatic routine requires an empty stage. Because balloons are released, this act should be performed in an enclosed space so that they can be retrieved.

LIGHTS: Bright daylight.

SOUND: Busy crowd noise may be used before actor appears. The clash of a cymbal is used several times. Carnival music may be used to accompany movements of the actor, and tape of the Wedding March may be used, but performance can be done without music.

PROPS: The performer carries a large collection of colorful balloons inflated with either helium or air. One balloon must be fully inflated with air so that it will pop when punctured. A pin or two secured in a cuff or lapel of performer's costume is necessary. The balloons may be secured to wands which are attached to a wrist ring or they may be fastened to a wire "top hat" worn by Gusto. They must be under control so that they can be released at a given moment.

COSTUME: Gusto wears a colorful and overstated clown costume. Clothing and shoes must not be an impediment, however, because of need for cartwheels and other gymnastics.

PLAYING TIME: Ten minutes. Time may vary depending on complexity of gymnastic routine.

CAST: One child and one teenager assisting from the audience are necessary, but Gusto is the primary character who appears on stage and may be male or female but must be an agile performer, preferably a gymnast who can do flips and cartwheels. At least he/she must be able to leap and bounce and execute a soft-shoe routine. The piece may be used as an opportunity for a sophisticated gymnastic performance but what the performer has to say is important. Gusto Buoyant is enthusiastic, fast moving, optimistic, even profound — not a typical sadfaced clown. The blending of motion and meaning should make the performance unique.

AT RISE: The stage is empty.

1   *(GUSTO enters in one or two great leaps, a bundle of inflated*
2   *balloons attached to wire top hat or secured on a wrist ring held high.*
3   *The clash of a cymbal is synchronized with his/her impact on the stage*
4   *floor.)* **Hey, hey, yo! Dreams for sale. Buy a dream here! A red**
5   **one! Blue! Yellow — the color of sun!** *(Cartwheels may be*
6   *synchronized with the following speech. Performer lets two or three*
7   *balloons go free.)*
8   **There! There goes spirit. There sails optimism. There rises**
9   **promise. Want to write on the sky? Want to soar like a song?**
10   **Buy a balloon. Purchase a promise! Buy a dream!** *(A CHILD*
11   *from audience hurries to the stage and pantomimes handing money*
12   *to GUSTO.)*
13   **What color, Buddy?** *(or "Princess")* **Green? Green for**
14   **gardens and trees and budding life? Green it is.** *(He pockets the*
15   *imaginary coin and hands a green balloon to the CHILD who returns*
16   *to audience, holding balloon securely.)*
17   **See, my buddy knows what he** *(she)* **wants. You let your**
18   **dreams tell you what you want. Balloons, you know, are just**
19   **bubbles of air. Bright ideas. We all know that. We all like them —**
20   **not just the kids. We all know that the real thing begins with**
21   **a dream. The balloons won't last long, but the dream can live**
22   **and grow right on into reality.** *(GUSTO executes a one-handed*
23   *cartwheel or puts the balloons aside and does a summersault. The*
24   *cymbal clashes as he lands. He takes several balloons from the packet*
25   *and holds them high as he dances across the stage in choreographed*
26   *leaps. As he touches down he pronounces each word of the following.)*
27   **Hope. Good job. Good health. Fame. New love. New car.**
28   *(He stops Center Stage, waving his balloons high.)*
29   **Dreams for tomorrow. Hope for things to change. Balloons**
30   **in all colors.** *(He stands stock still for a moment.)*
31   **We know they don't last. We know they will pop or slowly**
32   **collapse. We know that, but we want them anyway. A dream**
33   **is a parable. A dream is the bubble which can incubate reality.**
34   **A dream is the place to begin. A dream is a must, a treasured**
35   **possession. We need our dreams.** *(He allows another balloon to go*

1   *free.)*

2   **There you go! There rises an inflated promise — the pledge**
3   **of forever and ever. We know it's fragile, but we want it anyway.**
4   **We want to believe the balloon will always float, the color never**
5   **fade. We need the dream to pledge by. We have to begin.** *(He*
6   *crosses the stage in the halting step of the Wedding March, holding a*
7   *balloon at his waist, pantomiming a bouquet. Background music of*
8   *Wedding March may be used, or he may sing it — "Da da da-da. Da*
9   *da da-da.")*

10   **Or here is another.** *(He exchanges the "bouquet" balloon for*
11   *another and holds it high.)*

12   **Here now. Here is a dream. A college degree. A title. A**
13   **key to a career that can make all the difference. Who wants**
14   **that?** *(He holds it high and offers it to audience.)*

15   **You? You? Over there!** *(A TEEN runs toward stage and accepts*
16   *balloon, pantomimes the exchange of money, and runs back to*
17   *audience, holding balloon high.)*

18   **Now that was a bargain! A college degree on a stick! A**
19   **dream for a dollar. That's the way to do it. Kim** *(or student's*
20   *name)* **knows she has to keep that balloon pumped up. She**
21   **knows she has to read fifty pages of *Moby Dick* every day to**
22   **finish before the test. She knows she has to make the grades**
23   **to get the scholarship. She knows she has to have a summer**
24   **job. She knows her folks have to save, but *hey!*, it all starts with**
25   **a dream.** *(He takes out a red balloon. This one must be fully inflated*
26   *with air so that it will pop when punctured.)*

27   **How about this one? Red. Glorious red. Worth millions.**
28   **Say ten million? That's about right. It's the lottery. All you gotta**
29   **do is dream, right?** *(He does a soft-shoe shuffle with the red balloon*
30   *held high.)*

31   **Just buy a red balloon and a lottery ticket and you got it**
32   **made. Millions! A red Ferrari!** *(He pantomimes driving a sports*
33   *car, leaning back, head high.)*

34   **Two red Ferraris! Ten-room beach house. Rollicking on**
35   **the Riviera. Jetting to Jericho for a julep!** *(He struts with*

1   *imaginary drink in his hand.)*

2   **That's all you gotta do! Buy a red balloon!** *(He gestures with*

3   *a pin in his free hand and pops the balloon. Cymbal sound synchronizes*

4   *with balloon pop. He drops to his seat.)*

5   **Whoops! Something went wrong there. I got carried away.**

6   **Yep. I went too far on that lottery dream. Sorry.** *(He gets to his*

7   *feet.)*

8   **See, you gotta have a dream you can work on — like the**

9   **college degree. A lottery, now, you can dream, but you can't**

10   **win it a step at a time. You can't make it come true by**

11   **perseverance and planning. You can only waste your dream**

12   **money twice a week. Ever figure out how much ten dollars a**

13   **week adds up to with interest for ten years? You don't earn**

14   **interest on lottery tickets.** *(He takes out a yellow balloon.)*

15   **Here's one now that will come true. Yellow. Sunshine**

16   **balloon.** *(He swings it in a wide arc and dances across the stage with*

17   *it.)*

18   **This is the dream you can share with everybody in the**

19   **street. Can't hide sunshine. If it's there, it's for everybody.**

20   **Yellow for sunlight. Smiles. Hope. Some people stand right in**

21   **the light and never know it's shining on them. Some people**

22   **wake up in the morning and kick back nice warm covers,**

23   **stretch good sound muscles, sit down to bacon and eggs, and**

24   **don't even know their balloon is yellow. They go off to work**

25   **mad because they gotta work. Hey, I know someone who'll**

26   **change places with you any day. A cozy place to sleep where**

27   **nobody will step on you? Hot coffee and a regular paycheck?**

28   **Hey, you're floating a yellow balloon and don't know it. Smile!**

29   *(He lets yellow balloon go free.)*

30   **If you are living a dream and don't even know it, that's**

31   **for you. You just saw the sunlight!**

32   **One more now. Which color? Pink for a new baby? Gold**

33   **for a new job? Blue? Let's take blue. Blue is like this.** *(He waves*

34   *a blue balloon slowly, moving with it in wide arcs.)*

35   **Blue is for flying. We want to fly. We want everything to**

be sky-blue and clean and fresh and friendly. We want
unmarked sky. Fresh air — no garbage — no toxins — no
violence — no war.

We dream about good health and happiness and then
smoke a pack of cigarettes and curse the cough. We want the
landfill to disappear but we can't bother to recycle the pop
cans. We want relationships to last but try a little cheating for
kicks. We want peace in the world but fight over a bank balance
at home. We want the blue horizon but forget that we're
polluting atmosphere and attitudes all around us.

I think it's like this: We really want our dreams to fly. We
like the idea of being wafted away, like a balloon, from conflict
and anger and failure. We want to rise above it all, but the
other guy doesn't do it, so what's the use? We want the blue
balloon, but we don't want to pay the price. Because the price
means we have to clean up our own act.

We have to reach for the sky — for the dream. We have to
decide what we want and then work for it. *(GUSTO performs his
best acrobatic stunt. In the following speech he lets all the balloons go
free, one at a time.)*

There! Go to college! Keep the promise! Share the good
fortune! Turn in the pop cans! Navigate with spirit! Celebrate
success! Launch your dream! Reach for the sky! *(Sound of cymbal
as he lets last balloon go free and leaps Off-stage. Lights out.)*

16. ANDY ANDRIC

PRODUCTION NOTES

SET: A small table and chair are needed; family living room may be suggested.

LIGHTS: Interior daylight.

SOUND: No sound effects are necessary.

PROPS: Football, football helmet, video games, compact discs, fishing pole, baby stroller, shopping bags, packages, several large toys, toy truck, motor bike, shopping list, package of preemie diapers. Specific props and timing for their use are important.

COSTUME: Andy wears jeans, sweatshirt and running shoes or other casual clothing.

PLAYING TIME: Three or four minutes. Time will vary depending on extent of stage business.

CAST: Andy Andric* is a young father of twenty-five to thirty. He is so excited about his newborn son and his anticipated activities with him that he has gone to comical extremes to provide paraphernalia which he thinks will be needed for the child. A mood of enthusiasm prevails throughout the scene.

AT RISE: Andy enters Right and proceeds under a burden of packages and shopping bags to table about Center Stage. A fishing pole drags behind him. He holds a shopping list between his teeth. He lays his packages on table, chair and floor, calling out as he unloads.

* *andric: of or belonging to a male person.*

1   **Honey, I'm home!** *(Without removing shopping list from his*
2 *teeth, he tries to shout as if to someone on second floor.)* **Wait till you**
3 **see! I got everything on the list.** *(He takes it from his mouth, waves*
4 *it in triumph.)* **Diapers, bottles, bottle warmer — and a few other**
5 **things.**
6   **Hey, babies don't come cheap, do they?! That's OK. That's**
7 **OK. We'll get whatever he needs.** *(He unloads packages as he*
8 *speaks.)*
9   **Don't come down. Don't do it.** *(Still calling)* **Doctor said**
10 **you should take it easy for a few days. So stay put. I'll take**
11 **care of everything down here.**
12   **Got Andrew Michael III a couple of things.** *(He takes out a*
13 *very large toy truck.)*
14   **Think he'll like a dump truck? I always wanted one of**
15 **these.** *(He rolls it around the table top briefly but is eager to look over*
16 *everything and moves on quickly.)*
17   **How about a video game or two?** *(He takes these from*
18 *packages.)* **And a couple of CDs. "Bad Company" and "Mr. Big."**
19 *(Or he names two currently popular performers. He picks up fishing*
20 *pole, swings it as if casting.)*
21   **And we'll go fishing next spring. I'll teach him to cast soon**
22 **as he can walk.**
23   **Yeah, I got the bottles.** *(He takes them from shopping bags.)*
24 **He won't need these very long. Be eating steaks with me in no**
25 **time.** *(He takes out two or three large toys, experimenting with them*
26 *briefly, still talking to wife upstairs. Some ad-lib in naming items may*
27 *be necessary here, but his response to each is more important.)*
28   **Maybe we'll have to put some of these away until**
29 **Christmas, but might as well be prepared. Wait till you see all**
30 **this neat stuff.** *(He goes to Off-stage Right and brings in a stroller,*
31 *also loaded with packages.)*
32   **Got him a stroller, but he won't need that for long either.**
33 **He'll walk early.** *(He unloads stroller, pushes it around the room.)*
34 **Hey, how about that: front-wheel drive!** *(He returns to packages*
35 *on table and removes a football, assumes a stance for passing the ball,*

1   *then "catches" it and runs to opposite side of stage, tossing it from one*
2   *hand to the other.)*
3   **Little Buddy, we're goin' to make TDs as soon as you are**
4   **big enough to run.** *(He assumes several positions with the ball then*
5   *lays it aside.)*
6   **And you'll be needing this.** *(He takes out a helmet.)* **Hope it**
7   **won't be too big when you're ready.** *(He tries it on his own head,*
8   *takes it off.)*
9   **Not too soon for you to learn to aim for the big leagues.**
10 *(He calls upstairs again.)*
11   **Don't get up, Honey. Stay put. I got a lot of stuff, but I'll**
12 **bring it up and show you.** *(He stacks and organizes items as he*
13 *speaks.)*
14   **He won't need everything right now, but we'll have it on**
15 **hand.**
16   **Don't know why they think he's too small to come home**
17 **yet. All new babies are small.** *(He goes Off-stage and returns, rolling*
18 *a motor bike.)*
19   **Hey, Honey, I got him some wheels.** *(He sits on it and "rides"*
20 *it across Downstage, making motor sounds.)*
21   **What?** *(He listens toward "stairs.")*
22   **Oh, no. I didn't forget anything. Yeah, I got the preemie**
23 **diapers.** *(He parks motor bike, finds package of diapers, opens it,*
24 *holding up tiny diaper.)*
25   **Hey, you sure these preemie things are big enough?** *(Lights*
26 *go out.)*
27
28
29
30
31
32
33
34
35

17. MR. SMITH

PRODUCTION NOTES

SET: A classroom. A teacher's desk stands Center, facing audience. A chair stands behind the desk. A large chalkboard may be used Upstage Left of desk, but stage business associated can be pantomimed.

LIGHTS: Interior daylight.

SOUND: Off-stage sound of school passing bell is effective.

PROPS: A few worn textbooks, a stack of papers suggesting student work, chalk, eraser, class record book, note pad.

COSTUME: Mr. Smith wears a dress shirt without a tie, neat trousers (not jeans), nondescript but neat shoes, perhaps a sweater vest. His clothing is becoming and in fashion but not overstated.

PLAYING TIME: Nine minutes or less.

CAST: Mr. Smith is in his mid-forties or younger. Specific age is not important. He is good-looking, appealing, cheerful. He is a dedicated teacher and in no way stereotypical. He moves quickly, gestures with enthusiasm and energy, obviously enjoying his work and fine rapport with his students (audience).

AT RISE: Mr. Smith walks On-stage quickly as the tardy bell sounds and stops directly behind his desk. He speaks immediately to his students.

1   Good morning, ladies and gentlemen. *(Pause. He smiles.)*
2   OK, guys and girls. *(He takes a class record book and pen in hand*
3   *and moves across stage while scanning the audience as if checking*
4   *roll, glancing down six separate rows of seats. He moves quickly,*
5   *speaking almost to himself until the name of an absentee comes up.)*
6   Kenny, Melba, Donna, Art, Barney. Barney? Where's
7   Barney? *(He writes on a small pad on his desk.)* Nancy. Row two?
8   Everyone here in row two. Row three. Who's missing here?
9   Grenville. *(He writes on the pad.)* Four? OK. Five. All here. Six
10 all here.
11   Good. Only two people missing this morning. *(He walks to*
12 *Stage Left as he tears the top sheet from his note pad and reaches*
13 *Off-stage as if putting it on a hook outside the door.)* Hope Barney
14 and Grenville aren't down with the flu.
15   Oh, come on. *(Responding to someone in class)* You know
16 Barney and Grenville wouldn't go camping on a Friday
17 morning. Again. *(Mild sarcasm)*
18   But for the moment we are concerned with those who are
19 here. This is Friday and your essay assignment "For the
20 Environment and Me" is due. That's right. Right now, as a
21 matter of fact. Dig them up and pass them in while I read the
22 morning announcements. *(He picks up a sheet of paper and reads.)*
23   "Friday, May 17 *(or current date)*. Drama Club will meet
24 today during lunch period in room 212. Fourth-period teachers
25 please permit Drama Club members to leave four minutes early
26 for lunch line. Wilson Messenger reporters' meeting is
27 cancelled. Second-string football boys are to be excused from
28 seventh period for early practice." That's it. *(He "squares" a stack*
29 *of papers, puts them aside and comes around his desk and sits on it,*
30 *facing audience.)*
31   Now for this morning's quick wit exercise before we talk
32 about your next essay topic. There are thirty students in this
33 classroom and seven class periods per day. How many students
34 in this room per day? Per semester? Per year? Now, give or
35 take a few, number of students in this classroom in thirty years?

1   Oh, it's not intended to be an exercise in calculus, just
2   simple multiplication with a few assumptions. What did you
3   come up with? Right! Twelve thousand, six hundred students.
4   If one person teaches for thirty years in this high school (and
5   all factors remain constant) he or she will have met twelve
6   thousand, six hundred students.
7   "Overwhelming?" Sometimes, yes. Incredible always.
8   Well, no. I haven't taught for thirty years, but I would like to.
9   Mrs. Nooney has taught almost that long, and she remembers
10   the names of hundreds of people who were her students.
11   And I remember them, too, as long as you stay in your
12   seats. *(Laughs.)* Just kidding. I actually do know the names of
13   every student in all seven of my classes, and there are no two
14   of you alike.
15   Please conform a bit, Kevin, and sit with the back of your
16   chair behind you. It may be more interesting to straddle your
17   chair and rock back and forth, but it's safer as the designer
18   intended even if it inhibits your ingenuity. Ingeniuty and
19   inventiveness do not guarantee privilege. The natural laws do
20   apply to each of us even though each is an original. Sometimes
21   conformity is the wisest of choices and reflects individual
22   thinking. In other words, turn your chair around and sit on it.
23   *(Pause)* Thank you.
24   "Are we getting a lecture on individuality again?" Well,
25   Bonnie, we are going to talk about it. I want you to think about
26   human uniqueness as a choice for next week's essay assignment.
27   I never get over the fact that of all the students in this tenth-
28   grade class, this school, this district, in all the districts in the
29   state multiplied over and over again throughout the country,
30   the world, there are no two people alike!
31   Each one of you is extraordinary. You don't have to sit
32   backwards or let the laces of your high-tops dangle to be
33   different. You are different. Each inimitable. *(He walks around*
34   *the desk to the chalkboard and quickly draws [or pantomimes] a dozen*
35   *or more loops, squares, and rectangles, no two alike, illustrating while*

1   *speaking.)*
2   For some reason, the combination of cells and genes makes
3   it possible for every one of us to be different. It is even more
4   remarkable than singular telephone numbers for each
5   household and business in the country. We can create endless
6   combinations of numbers, but we can't come anywhere near
7   nature's record of unique human beings.
8   Yes, Wanda, "like the lottery." Endless combinations. *(He*
9   *returns to Downstage Center, speaks with clarity and emphasis.)*
10   "Are we being tested on this?" No, Paul, just let it sink in
11   before you start writing. Nature or God or the Creator seems
12   to have no trouble with this idea of individuality. I'm not giving
13   you a religious lecture here. Something created us all, whatever
14   or whoever — apparently fashioning each with intense
15   attention to our differences.
16   Does that suggest anything to you? Right! Each must be
17   important. Noteworthy. Significant. *(He prints the word*
18   *"significant" boldly on board.)* Maybe your essay title can be "I'm
19   significant."
20   That's it, Kenny. That's the point. Unique and apparently
21   as significant as we are, there are universal laws that apply to
22   all of us. *(He draws a circle encompassing the group of irregular*
23   *shapes.)* Gravity, for example. If we slip off the roof, we fall. If
24   we swallow poison, we die. That seems to suggest a direct
25   contradiction to my theory: the very antithesis of the concept.
26   Antithesis? *(He prints the word on the chalkboard.)* Think, of
27   it as two words: Anti thesis. *(He divides the word with a slash*
28   *mark.)* Go see old Mr. Webster if that doesn't explain it for you.
29   OK. If we are so individually significant, how come this
30   commonality of natural law? Why aren't we protected
31   individually? What do you think? If each of us is so special,
32   why can't we be exempt from illness and accident? From drug
33   addiction? AIDS? Drowning?
34   Are you getting an idea or two here for your paper? Are
35   we privileged because we are unique? Or does responsibility

1   go along with privilege? *(Pause)* You saw the news report on
2   TV about the boy over in Camport who shouted to his buddies
3   just before he tried to beat the locomotive to the crossing — "No
4   train can touch Tommy!" Many of us ignore responsibility and
5   natural laws out of a sense of personal privilege.
6   If you like to consider contradictions, we've got them here.
7   Why is it that we think, "It can't happen to me" or "That kind
8   of thing happens to the other guy — to the Smiths and Joneses?"
9   Right. To the Smiths and Joneses. *(Long pause)* My name
10 is Smith, as you know. There are millions of Smiths in the
11 world — each one unique. Well, do you know any Smith just
12 like your language arts teacher? *(He laughs forcefully.)* Mr. Smith
13 who doesn't misspell words or come late to class. Mr. Smith
14 who earned Best Teacher Award for two consecutive years.
15 Mr. Smith who never makes a mistake — in language arts class,
16 that is.
17   Well, let's clear up a few things here before you organize
18 your paper. Mr. Smith acknowledges his oneness as well as his
19 tendency to ignore universal laws. Mr. Smith didn't try to beat
20 a train to a crossing, but he did say, "It can't happen to me."
21 Mr. Smith, who would like to emulate Mrs. Nooney and teach
22 here at Wilson High School for thirty years, isn't going to have
23 the chance. *(He pauses, walks the width of the stage without speaking*
24 *and returns to Center Stage.)*
25   Mr. Smith is not even going to spend another semester
26 learning the names of two hundred more remarkable human
27 beings. *(Pause)* He — I — am not going to help you think up all
28 these challenging ideas for you to write about. *(Pause)* I will be
29 leaving Wilson High School soon. More specifically, at the end
30 of this week. *(He walks a few steps without speaking and pauses to*
31 *face audience steadfastly.)*
32   You see, instead of accepting the responsibility that goes
33 along with my uniqueness, I took a chance, and I was not
34 exempt from universal laws. *(He pauses as if struggling.)* I am
35 HIV positive. In fact, I have AIDS. *(Long pause)*

1   Remember that I was here, OK?

2   *(He is thoughtful as if speaking to himself.)* I won't be able to
3   look back in thirty years to say, "Yes, I knew her when." Or "I
4   remember a poem that famous man (one of you) wrote." I won't
5   be able to watch you all grow and share your talents with the
6   world. I won't be around in twenty years. Or ten. Maybe five
7   at best.

8   *(He speaks forcefully but calmly.)* But you will be. You will
9   be, that is, if you treasure your unique significance and respect
10   the natural laws which apply to all of us. If you realize that
11   you are responsible for your behavior — that you are important
12   enough to live.

13   Do you have an idea for your essay now? *(Pause)* Write a
14   good one.

15   Kevin, please don't trip over your shoe laces as you leave.
16   *(The passing bell rings and lights go out.)*

17
18
19
20
21
22
23
24
25
26
27
28
29
30
31
32
33
34
35

18. BRAWN

PRODUCTION NOTES

SET: A wild west bar. A typical swinging door Upstage Left is effective for Brawn's entrance, but the act can be done without it. A plank supported by two small ladders Downstage Center will serve as the counter and is important. A tall reader's stool can be used as a barstool.

LIGHTS: Low, mellow, evening interior. Smoke may be suggested.

SOUND: A cowboy tune, such as "Don't Fence Me In" or "Home on the Range" and sounds of tinkling glass may be used to introduce the act but should fade slowly as Brawn strolls about the stage. A cymbal clash is used to coincide with his entrance.

PROPS: None needed other than those included with costume.

COSTUME: Brawn wears a dirty, black cowboy hat, bandanna, dirty shirt, jeans with a wide leather belt, and well-worn cowboy boots. Holsters, complete with revolvers, are strapped to his shoulder and hips. His costume should suggest the sinister and dangerous man of the wild west.

PLAYING TIME: Two minutes.

CAST: Brawn is the stereotypical bad guy: threatening, mean, ominous. Scowl lines are over-emphasized and include an overstated handlebar mustache. His performance must be carefully calculated and controlled to create complete silence and audience attention before he speaks.

AT RISE: The stage is empty. Music diminishes.

1   *(With the clash of cymbal, BRAWN bursts through the swinging*
2   *doors Upstage, one hand on the revolver on his hip. He commands the*
3   *stage threateningly then stalks to Stage Left slowly, peering into*
4   *audience as if looking for someone. He then strides slowly across stage*
5   *to the Right, still surveying the scene menacingly. He may repeat this*
6   *routine until he has the complete, silent attention of the audience. Too*
7   *much stalking can elicit laughter and destroy the moment of revelation.*
8   *Timing is crucial to the effect the actor creates. He must anticipate*
9   *audience readiness.)*
10   *(Just right of the bar, he stops, removes one of his guns, swings*
11   *it around one finger, and studies a target in the audience. He then*
12   *returns the gun to its holster, takes out another gun, stepping backward*
13   *a few steps. Then he walks toward the bar and lays the gun on it.)*
14   *(With one hand on the gun in the shoulder holster, he straddles*
15   *the stool. He finally speaks in a manner completely in contrast to his*
16   *projected personality, to his costume, and to the audience's expectations.*
17   *His voice is modest, apologetic, high-pitched.)*
18   **May I have a Coke, please?** *(Lights go out.)*
19
20
21
22
23
24
25
26
27
28
29
30
31
32
33
34
35

19. NUNCIO

PRODUCTION NOTES

SET: Interior of a space shuttle at the control board. Down Center, a long, low table and one chair with a seat belt attached will serve.

LIGHTS: Stage is dark except for distinct focus on small area representing control room in shuttle interior.

SOUND: Suggestions of static from communications equipment between space shuttle and NASA ground control are needed.

PROPS: Headset transmitter and a heavy manuscript clamp "fastened" to the table. Three or four sheets of typed manuscript.

COSTUME: Nuncio wears cotton shirt and pants and boots with heavy soles.

PLAYING TIME: Nine minutes or less.

CAST: Nuncio* is a news anchorman and commentator who has been trained as a mission specialist for this space flight. This is his first trip in space. He is in his mid-thirties or older.

AT RISE: Nuncio enters Upstage Center and walks in calculated slow motion directly to Center Stage. He carries several sheets of a typed manuscript. He sits without moving the chair (to suggest that it is anchored) at table facing audience. He straps himself to chair and secures his manuscript to a clamp fastened to table. He grips headset as if dislodging it from its anchored position, slowly fitting and adjusting it. In pantomime he switches several controls on table top. Static is heard. He moves in slow motion throughout the act to suggest weightlessness in space. All movements must be carefully rehearsed. He listens carefully then speaks.

---

* *nuncio: hierarchical messenger.*

1   Messenger One to Houston. Shuttle Messenger One to
2   Houston ground control. Good morning, Houston. This is
3   Mission Specialist Nuncio aboard Messenger One. It is March
4   17, 1999, and we are into our second unscheduled orbit. I am
5   wide awake. Of course, you made a wake-up call, but we didn't
6   hear it. If you can't hear me — and I really doubt that you
7   can — my message will be on tape when we get back. If we get
8   back.
9   Commander Kelly is asleep. He needs it. He and Arnold
10   and Zulac have been working at the computer with their
11   calculations for about eighteen hours. Heimerman and Smith
12   have been trying to activate re-entry controls and repair our
13   damaged antenna since the completion of the scheduled
14   seventh orbit, as we have tried to report. I can't help them
15   much, so they let me take a nap. Well, I tried, but sleep isn't
16   what I need most right now.
17   These guys are incredible. Confident. Not awed by the
18   unknown. They're always "at ready" to learn something new.
19   How much can they take? Do you really have people prepared
20   and willing to spend six years on a round trip to Mars? Two
21   extra orbits just a few miles beyond that planned are unsettling
22   to a greenhorn like Mission Specialist Nuncio. There is more
23   to this than understanding the controls, that's for sure. *(He
24   pantomimes trying communications signals at the control board,
25   moving in slow motion. Static can be heard.)*
26   Houston, are you there? Come in Houston. Messenger One
27   to Houston. Messenger One orbiting out here somewhere. This
28   is Mission Specialist Nuncio, CBS anchorman, man of words if
29   not of courage, the man you trained to float around in space
30   and talk about it. *(He listens for a few seconds without speaking.
31   Sound of static.)*
32   You still don't read us. So. *(Pause)* So, I'll keep talking.
33   Taping. That was my assignment anyway — to report my
34   impressions of leaving Earth behind, of heading out into space
35   even on a trial run, of existing in a vacuum.

1   Of course we are supposed to know where we are at all
2   times, but that issue is a bit confused right now. We can see
3   Earth but we don't know exactly how far away we are. Computer
4   malfunctions are human error, of course, not equipment error.
5   But who put the decimal in the wrong place is not our main
6   concern at the moment.
7   Commander Kelly says we are orbiting at loosely two
8   hundred miles farther out than scheduled and in the ninth orbit,
9   although only seven were planned. But orbiting beyond
10 assignment wouldn't necessarily be a problem if all systems
11 were go — yours and ours.
12   But what is my response to this situation? I'm half excited,
13 half terrified. The unknowns are what shake me up. The rest
14 is absolutely exhilarating. Knowing that we are floating along
15 out here in a neutral celestial position like a bit of debris from
16 a planetary explosion of a billion years ago in no hurry to settle
17 anywhere — that part is fascinating. Makes me feel like a part
18 of the mystery — just a particle in the evolving universe — but
19 a particle.
20   The unknown is the frightening part. Why don't we read
21 you, NASA? Why don't you communicate with us? Have you
22 had an earthquake? Been struck by a tornado? When do we
23 get back on track? How do we get back? When do we go home
24 again? *(He tries controls again. Sound of static)*
25   This is Messenger One. Come in, Houston. Come in
26 Houston. Hey, you guys, where are you? *(He takes his manuscript*
27 *from the clip, handling it carefully in slow motion.)*
28   OK, if you won't talk, I will. My assignment. I'm to convince
29 the English speaking population of the world that humankind
30 is ready emotionally and intellectually — if not financially — to
31 cast off into deep space with a manned trip to Mars. I'm to help
32 persuade various congresses and other governing bodies
33 around the world to chip in a few billion each in a global effort
34 to add Mars to our conquest of space. So here we go. *(He clears*
35 *his throat, adjusts controls, and reads from his manuscript, gripping*

1   *it tightly. His manner is now that of the calm and experienced*
2   *professional.)*
3   Good evening friends around the world. From outer space,
4   orbiting Earth aboard U.S. Messenger One, on March 17, 1999,
5   this is Nuncio for CBS Cosmic Commentary. *(Brief pause)* For
6   generations beyond count, humankind, even since its most
7   primitive stage of development, has been reaching for the skies
8   and speculating about what is out there. We've wondered about
9   the stars since we first stood erect. For more than a thousand
10   years holy men thought of outer space and heaven as one and
11   the same — the ultimate home splendid beyond all our
12   imaginings.
13   Then yesterday there was Sputnik. What a jolt. It stirred
14   our emotions and determination. We learned how to rocket into
15   space, to orbit, and to return to Earth in dramatic style. We
16   made it to the moon in record time. We have sprinkled the sky
17   with satellites. We've accomplished nearly a hundred orbiting
18   missions and provided whole libraries of data to prepare for
19   explorations deeper into space — all within a brief moment in
20   human history.
21   We've made some mistakes. We lost Vanguard One and
22   its crew. We saw a Russian astronaut stranded for a year in
23   orbit. But knowing the chances we are taking, we press on into
24   the unexperienced.
25   There is much more to learn. What's out there is still a
26   mystery in spite of our space probe photos and calculations.
27   What's out there is still that unknown we've called heaven for
28   centuries, but it's bigger and much more mysterious than we
29   have yet imagined.
30   When I got my first glimpse of Earth, just after we went
31   into orbit a couple of hundred miles farther out than we had
32   planned, I experienced a sudden new perspective of the ancient
33   concept of heaven.
34   The splendor of blue Earth suspended there in delicate
35   balance in the continuing and changing and endless mystery

1   of the universe had such a profound impact on me that I will
2   never be the same again — whether or not I get back to it.

3   Earth is alive. It breathes, changes, evolves as we do,
4   accommodating generously to the needs of its inhabitants.
5   Earth, mysteriously suspended in all her majesty, is spinning
6   the multi-millionth time — one of the components making up
7   the ethereal whirlwind, a fragile element in the moiling,
8   exploding, spark-flying universe.

9   Somehow during millions of years constituting only a
10 moment of eternity, from the dust particles scattered on Earth's
11 surface, humankind has evolved and learned to call Earth
12 "home."

13   Here we are now with intellects developed to the point
14 that we bounce announcements off satellites to listeners
15 anywhere on the globe and beyond. We condense volumes of
16 information onto a microchip. We lift off with awesome power
17 to orbit the earth and celebrate our genius.

18   Here we are, technically proficient but unaware of our
19 responsibility in the scheme of all things. Here we are accepting
20 Earth as our home without recognizing its majesty, its
21 significance, and its fragility in the cosmos. Those ancient
22 philosophers and holy men didn't realize that their Earth was
23 a part of celestial geography, that their heaven was right at
24 their feet, that they were involved in the vast mystery which
25 includes us all. They didn't know that Earth is the very heart
26 of heaven itself. *(Pause)*

27   This is Mission Specialist Nuncio aboard Messenger One.
28 *(Pause)* **Good night.** *(He pauses, switches signals, stretches, and tries*
29 *once more to communicate with NASA. His voice no longer reflects*
30 *that of the professional commentator.)*

31   Messenger One to Houston. Hello, Houston. This is Mission
32 Specialist Nuncio aboard Messenger One. Do you read me,
33 Houston? Hey, Houston, where the hell are you? We wanna
34 come home. *(Static continues as lights go out.)*

35

20. STEWARD

PRODUCTION NOTES

SET: At about Center Stage stands a structure representing a rooftop. It projects just three feet above stage floor.

LIGHTS: Light should at first suggest early dusk. Toward end of scene it diminishes and a spot focuses on the speaker at Center Stage then fades out.

SOUND: The sound of raging flood water may be used at rise and at close of scene.

PROPS: Steward's pockets are stuffed with a wrapped hamburger sandwich and a red or yellow bandanna. A coil of rope is looped over one shoulder and secured around his chest. A mountain climber's hook dangles at the end of the rope. A functioning flashlight is hooked to his belt.

COSTUME: Steward wears an old baseball cap, a plaid shirt, a jacket with pockets, muddy, wet jeans, and loose rubber boots filled with muddy water.

PLAYING TIME: Seven or eight minutes.

CAST: Steward is in his fifties. He is powerfully built as if he has worked physically all his life. He is dirty and soaked and exhausted, but his voice is strong and vigorous.

AT RISE: The rush of flood waters is heard before lights go up, but the sound diminishes as soon as setting is established visually. Steward sits on rooftop with his head in his hands. He looks up then down, as if at water around him, and shouts.

1   Shut up you damned son of Satan! I've had to listen to
2   every filthy obscenity you've spit out for two weeks. Shut up,
3   you foul-mouthed monster! *(STEWARD shifts his position, takes*
4   *a large bandanna handkerchief from his pocket, removes his cap, wipes*
5   *his head and face, puts his cap on again, and stuffs the bandanna*
6   *back into his hip pocket. He is angry and tired.)*
7   Old Man River, my foot. You're no old man. You're a
8   colossal ogre vomiting into babies' cribs and all over the corn
9   flakes. You're a gorging gargantuan gobbling up furniture and
10   pets and farmers. You'd swallow the babies if you could. *(He*
11   *empties water from his boots and angles them upside down on the*
12   *edge of the roof.)*
13   You stop at nothing. *(He gestures widely.)* First you washed
14   out the beans, then the corn. Then you took down old Rusty.
15   What did you have against an old dog trying to help? Swept
16   him away like a broken twig. You'd have done the same to the
17   kids if I'd let them stay the night. My grandkids. My own flesh
18   and blood. *(He pauses, rubs his neck and legs as if exhausted. He*
19   *takes a wrapped hamburger from his jacket pocket and folds back the*
20   *paper, taking a bite.)*
21   Augh! Nothing is safe. *(Examining the sandwich)* Even
22   soaked my supper with your filth! Here, have my hamburger,
23   too. Take it all. *(He pitches the sandwich furiously Off-stage.*
24   *Carefully timed sound of splash in water can be used. He gingerly*
25   *stands and straddles the crest of the roof.)*
26   But not me. You're not going to take me. Keep playing
27   "You're next," but not me, Bozo, not me. *(He is still angry. He*
28   *swings the rope with hook on it.)*
29   I know you too well. You'll rage within an inch of my feet
30   all night if I have to stay that long, and when the sun comes
31   up, you'll laugh and giggle like a clown. You are not just a flood.
32   You're a knowing creature with stinking breath and putrid
33   fart. I used to laugh with you — especially at dawn — watching
34   the sun glisten on your surface. *(He gestures widely.)* You
35   laughed, all right, but I didn't know you were making fun of

1   me. *(He sits.)*

2   And look at me now. You heehaw and gulp down my fields
3   and vomit up mud and toxins and trees and disease. *(He sits.*
4   *He is calmer in his anguish. He wipes his face with his bandanna again.)*

5   Sue Mary tried to save the wedding pictures, all those
6   albums of the children and the grandkids, but they got soaked
7   in the bottom of the boat when you marked them with your
8   stinking piss. *(He holds his head in his hands and pauses then looks*
9   *up.)*

10   Highboy handed down four generations. Sue's pride and
11   joy. Collapsed. Just folded and gave up *(Gestures)*, floated plank
12   by plank around the living room. Grandma's china and
13   handmade quilts churned up with dead skunks. Books — even
14   the family Bible — like so much stinking garbage.

15   Bible. Yeah. Noah was warned. If God warned me, I didn't
16   hear him. Weather experts neither. They didn't tell us in time
17   to build an ark!

18   And my house won't float. It will hold for awhile, maybe,
19   but when this mess is over, it'll be half buried in dead dogs and
20   cows and fish and sewage. If it stands through the night we'll
21   be lucky. But what good will it be? Infested with snakes and
22   rats, rotting girders. Plaster turned to paste. Damn you! *(He*
23   *stands again, walks carefully with one foot on each side of the roof*
24   *crest. His voice rising, he gestures at the water again.)*

25   Thirty years I pussy-footed at your banks out of respect
26   for you. Told my kids to respect nature — God's river — the
27   continent's lifeline. What about my lifeline? My land? My
28   lifetime investments? You belching, nasty, selfish swine. *(He*
29   *wipes away a tear and sobs half in anger and half in despair.)*

30   Yeah, God. *(As if speaking to God, voice rising)* Why couldn't
31   you do something about this? I begged you. I prayed, loving
32   God and Father. Huh! About as caring as the river. About as
33   considerate. *(He stops to think for a moment, sits again, calms down*
34   *a bit.)*

35   OK, I'm trying to be fair. Trying to think it through. I'm

1 still alive. Sue Mary and the kids and the grandkids are high
2 and dry in the high school gym. Bill will be back before long
3 to take me in. I told him an hour more holding down my house.
4 As if I could. I know it can't be much longer. I'm supposed to
5 be thankful we are all alive. Except Rusty. Good, old Rusty.
6 And I can start again. *(Pause)* I guess, God, you start over
7 again with every seed and seashore every season. Yeah, I know
8 that. It's all a part of the cosmic cycle and universal intelligence,
9 but that doesn't make it any easier for this one ruined farmer.
10 This university-educated agronomist.
11 So, God. It's not doing much good to talk to the river. And
12 I wonder just at what level you hear what I have to say. I know
13 your answer: "You are still here, Steward. Start over. Why do
14 you think I made you in my image? Gave you a brain?" *(Pause)*
15 Go to church all my life. Live decently. Work. Work. Work. Give
16 all I can. Work some more. Give some more. Carry on with the
17 farm. Feed the world. Stewards feed the world. That's me,
18 Steward of the fields. *(Voice rising)* Then this monster snarls
19 and rises on his high haunches and wipes out everything.
20 Malignant monster. The River. God, you're not supposed
21 to be malignant, but hell, why do you let this happen, then?
22 Why? Why did you create each of us complete with intricate
23 DNA and independent spirit just to let a filthy, mindless river
24 destroy us? *(He pauses and shifts position. Lights dim slowly, begin*
25 *slow focus.)*
26 That's it. Mindless river. Symbol of life they said in lit
27 classes at State. Hah! Symbol of mindless power. Power out of
28 control. Wonder if the professor ever rode his house down the
29 river. *(Pause)* Well, I'm not riding. *(He visually estimates the*
30 *distance to imaginary water.)* Yet. But I will be if Bill doesn't show
31 up soon. Hope the motor didn't conk out. Use the flashlight if
32 it's after dark, he said. *(He puts on his boots as he continues.)*
33 Well, it's dark. This house is no boat. It's done the best it
34 could to hold out, but I can feel it dying beneath me. *(He stands.)*
35 But I won't die with it. I will hang onto something. *(He swings*

1   *the hooked end of the rope coil.)*
2   *(He alternately addresses God and convinces himself.)* **Loving**
3   **God?** *(Pause)* **Indifferent God? The river doesn't think.**
4   **Hurricane and earthquake don't think. But I can, and I get the**
5   **picture.**
6   **Cosmic intelligence speaks in a thousand voices, and the**
7   **message is clear. "I don't play favorites," says the Almighty.**
8   **"Take care of yourself. I've got the river to take care of. The**
9   **planet. The universe."** *(Lights slowly expand and dim. He speaks*
10   *thoughtfully.)*
11   **The human brain is part of the cosmic mind. My brain is**
12   **God's brain — or at least a little part of it. I'm supposed to**
13   **understand that the universal plan includes me only as part of**
14   **the total picture. What I accomplish within that frame is up to**
15   **me. Right?**
16   **So what am I doing sitting out here in the middle of the**
17   **Mississippi on top of my house cursing the mindless river? All**
18   **it can do is follow the cosmic rhythms.** *(He is very thoughtful,*
19   *thinking it out.)*
20   **I have to do that, too, but I can also try once more to take**
21   **care of myself.** *(His voice and confidence rise.)*
22   **So, I hear you, God. I'm listening. I know you're not going**
23   **to interrupt the ebb and tide to get me out of this. I know what**
24   **I have to do. I can do it.** *(Pause)* **If Bill shows up, that is.** *(Lights*
25   *dim slowly. STEWARD is silent for a moment, seems to be listening.*
26   *As the stage goes dark, he turns on his flashlight and arcs it slowly*
27   *above his head. He speaks in the dark.)*
28   **Don't hear the boat. Just the river. Hurry up, Bill. I don't**
29   **think my flashlight will attract much attention in heaven.** *(Sound*
30   *of rushing water increases. Flashlight arcs twice above the dark stage*
31   *before going out.)*
32
33
34
35

21. PROFESSOR SAVANT SAPIENCE

PRODUCTION NOTES

SET: The stage is empty except for a podium or lectern and a large chalkboard.

LIGHTS: Interior daylight.

PROPS: Chalk, lecture notes.

COSTUME: Professor Sapience is conservatively dressed in suit, white shirt and tie, and neat wing-tipped shoes. He wears spectacles on an elaborate chain or cord.

PLAYING TIME: Seven or eight minutes.

CAST: Professor Sapience is middle-aged. He speaks in a manner which suggests deep profundity, but what he says makes absolutely no sense. It is quite appropriate for him to refer to his notes. He enunciates with elaborate precision and gestures flamboyantly for no reason whatsoever. He regularly makes strong points with his chalk and frequently takes off his glasses and peers at the audience without obvious reason.

AT RISE: Professor Sapience walks on quickly, deposits his papers on the lectern, tapping them into shape, looks at the class (audience) over his glasses, and speaks.*

---

* *Some of the terms used in this piece are the courtesy of* Have a Nice Day — No Problem! A Dictionary of Clichés, *Christine Ammer, Plume, Penguin Books, 1992.*

1   Good morning, ladies and gentlemen. I hope you have had
2   your morning exercise and nutrients, for today we begin an
3   attention-demanding unit on logic and thought. Every word is
4   important. Take notes. Pre-cise notes. *(He emphasizes syllables.)*
5   Try to understand as we move along. You will be examined on
6   this material.
7   Our topic is original thought. Be it understood. Or-i-gin-al
8   thought. *(He emphasizes each syllable.)* We are going to examine
9   the concept that original thought is the only valid thought. All
10   else is imitation. We will not imitate. We will think. We will be
11   original. Listen carefully to what has been established by the
12   experts. *(Throughout the "lecture," the PROFESSOR uses the*
13   *chalkboard frequently, quickly writing or printing words that make*
14   *no point whatsoever. After each third word, he underlines boldly with*
15   *a flourish.)*
16   To begin with, we know that ignorance is bliss. *(He quickly*
17   *prints "bliss" on the board.)* But wisdom is a horse of different
18   color. *(He removes his glasses and peers at the audience to make his*
19   *point.)* Be it understood.
20   First point. Fundamental truth: Horse sense. *(He prints*
21   *"horse.")* An ill wind blows no one any good. Or more simply,
22   in a nutshell, you haven't got a Chinaman's chance if you start
23   with a raw deal. The rank and file know-it-all *(He prints "rank")*
24   knows nothing without indexed and referenced proof.
25   It's not talking through your hat to talk turkey about a
26   theory — take note — so well understood. *(He prints "hat.")* Now,
27   as a matter of fact, you don't have to be a walking encyclopedia
28   to know the ropes and knuckle under to achieve in this field
29   of endeavor. *(He repeats business with glasses.)*
30   It's pure and simple intuitive, original knowledge. Be it
31   understood. Prove your point thereby. Stand your ground and
32   stand up and be counted. You will start off on the right foot.
33   *(He prints "foot.")* Then you'll soon steal the thunder of the less
34   well-informed. You know that necessity is the mother of
35   invention, so, when necessary, refer to mother. Just speak the

1 **naked truth.** *(He shapes squares with his hands and arms, not the*
2 *anticipated rounded body shape suggested by "naked.")*
3   **Second point: Speak for yourself. Speak your mind. You**
4 **will be speaking the same language as that of the experts.** *(He*
5 *prints "mind.")* **Your reasoning will be as sound as a bell. Stick**
6 **to your guns from stern to stern.** *(He gestures awkwardly.)*
7   **If you steal a march on other experts** *(He prints "march")*,
8 **so much the better. The name of the game is that they are**
9 **running on empty. They are run-of-the-mill. There's no fool like**
10 **an old fool.** *(Repeats business with glasses.)*
11   **Point three: In searching for profound truth, be it**
12 **understood, you will have the best of both worlds.** *(He prints*
13 *"worlds.")* **The uninformed will be at loose ends, all at sea, at**
14 **the crossroads, at the end of their rope.**
15   **At this juncture it will be child's play to defeat them at**
16 **their bag of tricks. They'll have to go back to square one or**
17 **back to the salt mines and start from scratch. They won't be**
18 **able to get your back to the wall.**
19   **The ball is in your court** *(He prints "court" and repeats the*
20 *business with his glasses)* **where you lay out your facts. Facts. A**
21 **ball-park figure is close enough to begin your battle royal. The**
22 **be-all and end-all will be as clear as a bell.** *(He prints "bell.")* **Be**
23 **it understood.**
24   **Those without your expertise won't see the forest for the**
25 **trees.** *(He studies his notes.)* **Oh, I'm sorry, that's "the trees for**
26 **the forest." We must be accurate. Precise. You'll be in the**
27 **catbird seat from day one. Day one, that is.**
28   **Catch as catch can is better than being caught with your**
29 **pants down, so always be Johnny-on-the-spot. You'll never**
30 **have to change your tune when the chips are down.**
31   **Point four: That's number four. Of course you must start**
32 **each day with a clean slate, clear the air, and count your lucky**
33 **stars. You must play your cards with care. Come hell or high**
34 **water, don't give up ship in midstream. Make short work of**
35 **each task.** *(He prints "hell," a slash mark, and "high" and draws*

1   *meaningless arrows from one word to another.)*
2   Your long suit will be in locking horns with the pretended
3   experts. Whoever said that a little learning is a dangerous thing?
4   Live and learn, I say. Live and let live.
5   There's always a light at the end of the tunnel, so don't
6   let the grass grow under your feet. Bend over backward or you
7   won't have a leg to stand on. *(Pause. He repeats the business with*
8   *the glasses.)* Lay it on the line! You can laugh out of the other
9   side of your face and cry all the way to the bank *(He prints*
10   *"bank")* when the die is cast on the day of reckoning.
11   Final point, point number five: You'll be dead right and
12   fancy free if you keep your nose clean and keep your powder
13   dry. You will keep a stiff upper lip in all lines of diversity and
14   keep your head above water. You'll not be a Johnny-come-
15   lately or a Jack-of-all-trades, but a Johnny-on-the-spot. *(He*
16   *prints "spot" and follows it with heavily marked dots to the edge of*
17   *the board.)*
18   It's a small world, and you have a place in it. In the long
19   run, you'll be in the pink, in the saddle, and in the swim. *(He*
20   *prints "swim.")*
21   In this day and age you can't reinvent the wheel, so stick
22   to what you know best. In point of fact it's in the cards that
23   you'll be on the inside track in no time. You'll be in the driver's
24   seat, in the groove, in the limelight.
25   In a word, speak up in no uncertain terms about what you
26   know. In a nutshell, without ifs, ands and buts, you'll have it,
27   hook, line and sinker. The uninformed won't hold a candle to
28   you, so don't hide your light under a bushel.
29   You'll be a hard act to follow. Hang in there. *(As he speaks*
30   *he draws bold lines and sharply emphasized arrows and circles in no*
31   *particular pattern.)* Sink your teeth into it. Keep your chin up
32   and your powder dry. Keep the show on the road.
33   Think   profoundly.   *(Business   with   the   glasses)*   Think
34   originally. O-rig-in-a-lly. *(Emphasizes each syllable then looks at*
35   *his notes.)* That's Or-i-gin-al-ly.

1   **And that's the bottom line. Be it understood.**

2   **Test on this vital material next time.**

3   **Have a nice day.** *(He gathers up his notes and walks briskly*

4   *Off-stage.)*

5

6

7

8

9

10

11

12

13

14

15

16

17

18

19

20

21

22

23

24

25

26

27

28

29

30

31

32

33

34

35

Myron LeRoy as "MACK"

22. MACK

PRODUCTION NOTES

SET: The interior of the cab of a huge truck/tractor rig. A cab seat may be suggested by a bench elevated in some way to give the impression of height. A steering wheel which actually turns is useful, and some kind of foot support is needed to allow for braking, but pantomime of driving business can be very effective. The seat may face the audience directly or may be off-centered and at an angle.

LIGHTS: Daylight, exterior. Focus on cab. Red flood near conclusion.

SOUND: Sound of interference on the CB channels may be used but is not mandatory.

PROPS: A hand-held CB microphone and a fire extinguisher of the type used in a truck cab.

COSTUME: Mack wears typical trucker's clothing: well-worn boots, jeans, flannel shirt, winter jacket, baseball cap or cowboy hat.

PLAYING TIME: Ten minutes.

CAST: Mack is the only character who appears, but in his speech he relays the presence of two other truckers. He is relaxed, friendly, and an experienced, well-trained driver anywhere between forty and sixty-five. He has a pleasant, deep voice and, even in emergency, a calm manner which by contrast emphasizes the tense situation which occurs.

AT RISE: Mack is driving. He pantomimes the handling of the wheel, gears, foot controls, and outside mirror. This stage business should be carefully controlled and rehearsed. He speaks to a buddy over his CB mike.

1   Ah, dispatcher says, we got a dandy. Got a load of frozen
2   potatoes. So I went down to Hermiston there at Ore-Ida, picked
3   up a load of French fries, took 'em back to Sumner to Gold
4   State Foods. Actually McDonald's. Stayed on that French fry
5   run for a week straight. That's all I did for a whole week was
6   haul French fries from Oregon back to Sumner. Finally got a
7   little bit tired of that, so I said, "You got anything new?"
8   Dispatcher says, "OK, we got a load of spaghetti sauce outta
9   Merced." Went to Merced to Ragu Spaghetti Sauce. Picked up
10   a load of sauce, headed for Portland. Dropped that load. Came
11   back to the terminal. I'd been out two weeks and five days away
12   from home. He gave me two days. 'Bout enough time for a
13   shower and a nap.
14   Been to Salty since then. Load of T.P. Then down to Reno
15   haulin' salt. Played the slot machines a bit. Went to bed early.
16   Like to git an early start when we're goin' over Donner in
17   weather like this. Yeah, Reno's always kinda fun.
18   Hold on, Go Devil. Met a new guy at the truck stop at
19   Boom Town. He wanted to rap a bit on eighteen before we git
20   to the top. I'll check in with him and get back to ya. Over. *(Sound*
21   *of radio frequency interference may be used as he switches CB channels.*
22   *Pantomime of driving details is carefully done. Some shifting of gears*
23   *without a lot of attention drawn to it lends reality. He drives as he*
24   *speaks.)*
25   That you, Hensley Cross-Country? Pack Horse here. Red
26   Universal cab — over. Pack Horse to Hensley Cross-Country.
27   *(Pause)* Yeah. Talked to you back in Boom Town. What's your
28   handle? Kick 'er back. *(Pause)* Yorki? Yorki as in New York?
29   Outta the Big Apple? Long ways from home. What's your twenty
30   now? Over to you.
31   I'm about ten miles ahead of you. Headin' for San
32   Francisco? Shaky Town. Me, too. "How far?" Well, 'bout five
33   hours. Straight up for a few miles and then straight down the
34   rest of the way. Well, not exactly straight. Windin' and sharp
35   grades, as a matter of fact. You made this run before? No? Well,

1 wanna run together? Real interesting goin' up over the pass.
2 Came the other way a couple of weeks ago. Cold and
3 windy. Snow and ice. Had the chain signs out. Had to throw
4 iron. Maybe not this time. Stick with me. Ain't easy, but once
5 you done it, it's no problem.
6 No, not much traffic if you're thinkin' New York City, but
7 plenty for climbing up and crawling down the other side. What
8 you haulin'? Makes a difference, 'specially goin' down. Over.
9 Auto supply? Twenty-four tons? Me, a load of salt to take
10 over to Shaky Town. Pick up computers and stuff for Radio
11 Shack, head back to Portland.
12 Have any trouble at Reno chicken coop? They sure don't
13 want no overload goin' over Donner. Want yer load controlled
14 and yer speed at double nickels or less. Less most of the time
15 on the way down. Lots of windin'. Fun, but gotta be careful.
16 Hold on awhile, Yorki. Gotta check on my partner, Go-
17 Devil. He's out there ahead of us somewhere. I been gettin' him
18 on seventeen. We make this run together regular. Hold on. Over.
19 *(He changes channels. Sound of frequency interference may be used*
20 *with each of these changes.)*
21 Pack Horse here to Go-Devil. Pack Horse to Go-Devil. Hey,
22 buddy, what's your twenty? Kick'er back.
23 What's your hurry? You're nearly to the top. You really
24 got yer hammer down. Let 'er coast till we catch up to you — me
25 and the new kid.
26 Yeah, we got a new boy on the run today. Been talkin' to
27 him on eighteen. Behind me about ten. Never done Donner
28 before. Loaded with auto parts. Handle of Yorki. Yeah, outta
29 the big city. Asks lotta questions. Might need a little guidance
30 once he's over the top. Copy? Over. *(He concentrates on driving,*
31 *switches channels.)*
32 Pack Horse callin' Yorki. Pack Horse here. How you doin',
33 Yorki? Kick'er back.
34 Well, no, not quite ninety degrees up. Real climb, though.
35 Good road. No chain signs yet. Must've melted last couple of

1   days.

2   No, that don't mean there ain't no ice. Lots of patches, but

3   you don't need chains to maneuver. Just don't hit yer brakes

4   on a patch of ice. Hold down yer speed. Take it real easy. This

5   ain't rain. It's ice comin' down. Not bad, though. Keep your cool.

6   What's the trouble? You sound a little anxious.

7   You didn't know this hill was quite so steep? This ain't no

8   hill, Yorki. This is a mountain, and we ain't even to the top yet.

9   Yeah, you climb a little, drop a little, then climb again. You'll

10   know it when you start down the other side.

11   Hang in there and round off those curves real easy. Almost

12   to the top, couple more miles, then down. Use your lowest gear.

13   Hug the fog line. Don't try to pass nobody. Let them pass you.

14   You're doin' fine, buddy. Over. *(He switches channels.)*

15   Pack Horse to Go-Devil and everybody else chattin' on

16   seventeen. Think we might need real attention on seventeen.

17   You guys let me and Go-Devil have a clear channel for a few

18   minutes? Thanks, buddies.

19   Go-Devil, this kid's scared to death. Don't know how to

20   drive over a mountain pass. Slow down a bit in case I need

21   you. Hold tight at about the summit. If he thinks it's tricky

22   going up, wait till he starts down.

23   Good. Thanks for clearin' the line, dudes. This ice rain

24   ain't designed for no cocktails. It's really comin' down. Too late

25   for puttin' on chains. Yeah, I think I can see his nose now and

26   then. He's gainin' on us and rollin' kinda loose, seems to me.

27   Don't know nothin' about mountain drivin', coaxing a rig down

28   the slopes. *(He checks rearview mirror.)*

29   Yeah, we're at the top. He made it this far. Over. *(He switches*

30   *channels, uses rearview mirror.)*

31   Pack Horse to Yorki. We're at the summit, buddy. *(Pause)*

32   What? "Ten-thirty-three?" Don't play games, man. What

33   emergency? Yeah, we're at the top. You're right behind me. I

34   can see your grille. *(Pause)* Yer brakes are smokin'? Man, we

35   ain't even started down. If you're smokin' already you'll never

1   be able to stop by the time we get to the bottom. *(He is still calm,*
2   *speaks without excitement.)*
3   Hold on, kid. I'll get my buddy to help. We'll git out ahead
4   of you and see if we can clear a path. There's an escape ramp
5   down here about three miles. You can make her. Get a grip on
6   it. Over. *(He switches channels.)*
7   Pack Horse here to Go-Devil. The kid's ten-thirty-three,
8   burned up his brakes. Git over to the fog line and put the
9   hammer down. I'll pull up beside you, keep the traffic herded
10   ahead. Maybe we can stay ahead of him. *(He pantomimes some*
11   *careful maneuvering to get cars to pass him.)* Atta boy. Go on
12   around, Mr. Cadillac.
13   If all we get is a speedin' ticket from Smokey we'll be
14   lucky. I'd like to git to Shaky Town fer supper. I'd like to git
15   anywhere fer supper. Hug the fog line, Devil. Here I come. *(He*
16   *pantomimes pulling his truck ahead beside Go-Devil, watches Yorki*
17   *behind him. Speed of speeches picks up.)*
18   And here he comes. I can see the front of his mule's cab
19   and smoke off his brakes. He must be ridin' his brakes. Hit yer
20   horn and hold it there. Nobody tryin' to pass him, that's fer
21   sure. I'm hittin' seventy-five even on the curves. Buddy, he's
22   losin' her back there. He's gainin' on us.
23   They're not pullin' out ahead of us fast enough. Punch the
24   panic button. They gotta git outta the way. Think we're playin'
25   games, I guess. Keep 'em movin'. Keep 'em movin'. Get back to
26   ya. Over. *(He switches channels, concentrates on curves, on truck next*
27   *to him and on outside rearview mirror. He is tense but his voice stays*
28   *calm.)*
29   Pack Horse to Yorki. Pack Horse to Yorki. OK, Yorki. I
30   see ya. Ya got a little over a mile to cover before the escape
31   ramp. Concentrate on the curves. Yer goin' too fast to change
32   gears, so just hang on. One mile. When you get to the ramp,
33   just let her climb on her own. It'll take you straight up. Yeah,
34   you're really movin' but you're OK. Don't use no gas or brakes
35   on the ramp. We're doin' the best we can to keep traffic movin'

1   down ahead. You just concentrate on huggin' the road and
2   watchin' for the ramp. I'll be right back. Over. *(He switches*
3   *channels, checks truck beside him, uses mirror.)*
4   Pack Horse to Go-Devil. Ten-thirty-three. Ten-thirty-
5   three. Keep movin'. Keep movin'. I could hand you a cup of
6   coffee if we had time. He's gainin' on us, but he's got to make
7   it to the ramp. It ain't smoke — just plain fire. Fire on wheels.
8   Get your extinguisher ready. He's just ready to hit the ramp.
9   He made it! He's on the ramp! Look at him climb that
10   mountain. He must be goin' up at sixty. Whooie!
11   We kin slow down now. No! Don't let her slide! Stay over
12   there, Devil! Git ahead of me before you pull out. Stop when
13   you can and come back with your extinguisher. Over. *(He*
14   *switches channels, watches every direction.)*
15   Pack Horse to Yorki. Yorki, you made it! You're doin' fine.
16   Soon as you get to the top, your rig will stop. Soon as you can,
17   jump out. You're on fire, so jump when you're down to about
18   thirty. Just fly and roll away from the rig.
19   We'll stop soon as we can and come back to put out the
20   fire. Do you read me, Yorki? No matter. Just do it. Down to
21   fifty? Git ready, man. Down to forty? Open the door! Atta boy!
22   Down to thirty! Jump!
23   He made it! *(He switches channels.)* He made it! He jumped.
24   He's rollin' a bit. *(Red flood light envelopes stage.)*
25   There she goes! Whoof! The devil! His rig's exploded. Balls
26   of fire! Yorki's gettin' on his feet. Slow down, Devil, and git
27   stopped. Git your extinguisher and run. Over. *(He switches*
28   *channels, speaks calmly.)*
29   Ten-thirty-three. Rig C.M. 121 to Donner patrol. Rig C.B.
30   121 to Donner State Highway Patrol. This is Mack Jensen on
31   C.M. 121. Ten-thirty-three. We got a fire up here on the escape
32   ramp three miles west of the summit. Git us some help. Over
33   'n out. *(He grabs his fire extinguisher, leaps from the cab, and runs*
34   *off stage shouting.)*
35   Comin' Yorki! *(Lights go out.)*

Overture
HALOS and HATS

by Dana Libonati

Scene Change Music 1

by Dana Libonati

Scene Change Music 2

by Dana Libonati

Scene Change Music 3

by Dana Libonati

ABOUT THE AUTHOR

Photo by Shirley J. Adams

Rachael C. (Ballenger) Burchard, literary critic, poet, and playwright, has taught in middle school, high school, and university. She is the mother of four and lives and writes in McMinnville, Oregon. She is the author of *John Updike: Yea Sayings*, Southern Illinois University Press, 1971 and 1974. Her poetry has appeared in anthologies, journals, little magazines, and a volume, *Green Figs and Tender Grapes*, Wyndham Hall Press, 1985. *Hallelujah Hopscotch*, a children's play, Coach House Press, 1986, and Dramatic Publishing Co., 1989, has entertained children throughout the country. Collections of monologs, *We the Real People, We the Real People II,* and *Troupers and Tramps* are published by Meriwether Publishing Ltd., Contemporary Drama Service (1989, 1991, 1994).

ORDER FORM

MERIWETHER PUBLISHING LTD.
P.O. BOX 7710
COLORADO SPRINGS, CO 80933
TELEPHONE: (719) 594-4422

Please send me the following books:

_____**Troupers and Tramps #TT-B148** $10.95
       by Rachael C. Burchard
       A collection of one-person plays

_____**Playing Scenes — A Sourcebook for**
       Performers #TT-B109 $14.95
       by Gerald Lee Ratliff
       How to play great scenes from modern and classical theatre

_____**Scenes and Monologs From the Best**
       New Plays #TT-B140 $14.95
       edited by Roger Ellis
       An anthology of new American plays

_____**The Scenebook for Actors #TT-B177** $14.95
       by Norman A. Bert
       Great monologs and dialogs for auditions

_____**Scenes That Happen #TT-B156** $10.95
       by Mary Krell-Oishi
       Dramatized snapshots of high school life

_____**Winning Monologs for Young Actors #TT-B127** $10.95
       by Peg Kehret
       Honest-to-life monologs for young actors

_____**Truth in Comedy #TT-B164** $12.95
       by Charna Halpern, Del Close, and Kim "Howard" Johnson
       The manual of improvisation

These and other fine Meriwether Publishing books are available at your local bookstore or direct from the publisher. Use the handy order form on this page.

I understand that I may return any book
for a full refund if not satisfied.

NAME: _____

ORGANIZATION NAME: _____

ADDRESS: _____

CITY: _____ STATE: _____ ZIP: _____

PHONE: _____

☐ **Check Enclosed**
☐ **Visa or MasterCard #**_____

                                Expiration
*Signature:*_____ *Date:*_____

(required for Visa/Mastercard orders)

COLORADO RESIDENTS: Please add 3% sales tax.
SHIPPING: Include $1.95 for the first book and 50¢ for each additional book ordered.

☐ *Please send me a copy of your complete catalog of books and plays.*